# Accept Who You Are

*And Witness Your Reality Transform*

# Accept Who You Are

*And Witness Your Reality Transform*

Natasha Sumner

ISBN-979-8-9992656-0-9

Dedicated to my dear mother, Donna Shury; the warm, nurturing soul who taught me about the transformative power of unconditional love, and Patti Intoranat – the soulmate and friend that has positively and profoundly impacted my journey.

# Foreword

Imagine opening a printed work and picking up, in one text, much of what you need to know to graduate from the University of Life. That would also be a mighty fast accomplishment... and that's what you could well experience when you turn the final page of this book.

Seldom have I seen as much incredibly valuable, right-on-the-money observations, insight, and advice as I found in each chapter of Accept Who You Are by Natasha Sumner. If you want a short course that could take you a long way, you're looking at it right now.

~ Neale Donald Walsch

*The sun took refuge in the twilight...*
*The dazzling lights that tantalize fade...*
*The dark will creep in soon to shroud all that is of the light...*
*The eye turns inward, do you see me now?*

*The tongues wag, the ego clamors for attention...*
*A mad rush to fill the void, squirming in the silence...*
*A jab, a death, a shock to the system...*
*The mental chatter slows, do you hear me now?*

*Feet a-marching to the noiseless beat of a pavlovian drum...*
*The dancer grows tired of the dance...*
*He glances back and sees his strings...*
*A silence sets in, do you feel me now?*

*Souls jostling for affection and acknowledgement*
*Love loses meaning as beyond the grasp of the mind...*
*Scattered reflections, how could Source not love itself?*
*The heart expands, do you remember me now?*

- *An Ode to Self*

# Table of Contents

# Prologue

Have you ever felt like you're different? Not different as in lacking ten fingers and toes, walking through walls or somersaulting off-of-a roof kind of different. Not that these things aren't possible, but this is not the difference of which we speak. In fact, the difference alluded to cannot be qualified in words. It comes up as a feeling – better yet a knowing. You've always been different. It's something you've always known.

For as long as you can remember, they've called you all kinds of names. *Black sheep, dreamer, loner, oddball, misfit, upstart, renegade, outlier, autistic.* You name it, you've heard it. Any label that could justify the anomaly of who you are. When these boxes no longer seemed to fit, they came up with more elaborate names, or worse yet, diagnosed you with afflictions that no amount of talk therapy, pills or poppers could fix.

With time, the boxes grew bigger, enshrouding you in their makeshift world. And you remained a part of that reality for as long as you believed them. Until you did not.

There was always that little nagging voice in your head, whispering to you for as long as you were willing to hear it. Entreating you that you were something more. What or who, you did not know. But you knew what you were not.

So, at an early age, you rummaged through books – as many books as you could find, and meandered through life...the relentless seeker, the silent watcher, looking for some clue to the puzzle of who you are. You felt that if you looked deeply enough, listened attentively enough, read extensively enough, felt fully enough, cried softly enough, laughed spontaneously enough and loved passionately enough...you'll uncover a clue; a clue that explained your existence.

There were many little clues along the way. Moments where time stood still, and your heart pounded erratically in your chest for no particular reason. Like the *DeJa'Vu* that took hold upon stepping foot in a place that you've never before visited or locking eyes with a complete stranger... when every fiber of your being hummed with familiarity.

Or that moment where you felt like you plummeted into a brick wall and hit rock bottom, except visually there was no wall or rock, so no one was going to believe you if you told them anyway.

But you certainly felt it and continued to revel in the poignancy of the moment long after that; much after you were catapulted back to the present reality. But wait a second – why did that moment feel more real than anything you'd ever experienced, why did you feel so much more alive than before?

In the space that straddled that moment and the one that followed it, where everything stopped and the mind for the first time snapped out of its analytical frenzy – you'd never before experienced that degree of peace, presence and clarity felt. It was like the entire

Universe had stopped its agenda to dialogue with you, and every cell in your body perked up to attention as if in the presence of something transcendental. In a space of no words, you were given a fleeting glimpse of something quite magical.

It left no doubt that there was something much larger, much grander than yourself that existed, and that it and you were one and the same. *It was outside of you, yet a part of you. It was larger than you, yet within you.* Your mind swirled and resumed its usual chatter, trying to attribute meaning to the experience. Slicing and dicing to extract the logic – something concrete that it could hold on to, something to unravel the mystery... to decode the truth.

The truth of who you are – that clue, lurked right around the corner. You could feel it. You are so close to discovering the missing puzzle piece that is going to make your entire story fall into place. You're so close to unveiling and unshrouding the truth of your identity. Why? Did you think it is by coincidence that you've picked up this book and pulled apart the pages?

# *1*

# *Who are you, Divine Soul?*
## *Do you even know who you are?*

Now that you are here, let's start from the beginning....

The starting point. Which you may imagine to be as a baby...kicking and crying as you emerge from your mother's womb; a tiny bundle surrounded by a sea of curious faces, probing eyes, masked visages of the nurses and doctors barking instructions; a yell, a grin, a joyful outburst.

Feet dangling, you're held up for the world to see, probed here and there to see if you passed initial inspections ...a toe, a limb...all in the right place, before placed back into the arms of one that stares at you in the most intimate way. It's all a blur; the sights, the sounds, the smells, the feel of the air against your skin, their hands... her hands. What a world!

And this is a very good start, except we're venturing much beyond this. Before even this memory which, it would be reasonable to presume that you do not yourself have – apart from what was gleaned from that faded picture or video shot ions ago. An enthusiastic attempt to commemorate that moment; tickling stories passed along by those that bore witness to your birth. But is the moment of your birth actually where your story began?

Could it be when you were conceived? Feeding the patriarchal conceit of the valiant sperm racing down a fallopian canal to invade and conquer the passive and recipient ovum awaiting it. Or even before that?

What if we were to imagine for a moment a different starting point; a different point of exploration from which to begin? Without making any inferences; leaving all preconceived notions at the door. Your mind too... let's park it for a bit. You can retrieve it later, as where we are venturing is beyond the reach of the mind.

The only thing you'll need is your imagination. The fact that you are reading this book tells me you likely have a very active one. So come along now. Let's begin our exploration. I dare say, by revisiting the excerpt below...

*In the beginning, the earth was without form and a void, and darkness was upon the face of the deep. And God said, let there be light, and there was light. And God saw the light, that it was good.*

*'But this is from the bible'*, your mind protests with frenzy. What if I'm not religious? What does a phrase from an old scripture somewhere have to do with who I am? Yet it has everything to do with unravelling your story...and at the same time nothing. As this is far from a religious exploration.

Even so, regardless of what you believe in, be it... *God, Krishna, the Universe, science, nature...* whether you are agnostic, a Buddhist, or do not believe in anything at all, we can all agree that there is a Universe of which we are a part. So, if it helps to replace the word *God* with *Universe* or science, by all means do so.

Now, momentarily close your eyes and allow your gaze to rest upon the abyss of darkness behind your eyelids. See it as a dark void, stretching in every direction, as far as the inner eye can see. It's pitch black — a unifying and singular darkness. Within the makeshift universe of your inner kingdom, it is all there is.

Being all there is, it transcends all spaces, every nook and cranny within the imponderable depths of your mind's eye. Being all there is, this limitless void; this singular consciousness, also has no experiential awareness of itself.

Adrift within a cosmogenic sea of experiential oblivion, as you were in the primordial moments that preceded your birth – immersed within the amniotic waters of your obscure, prenatal world. Yet if all you ever experienced, no matter how far or long you floated was pitch-darkness, would you have an awareness of anything else? Or what you looked like? Fingers? Hands? Toes?

Beset with an intense desire to better know itself, this consciousness differentiated itself from the darkness, creating light; a burst of color sprang forth, birthed from the depths of its imagination. The light irradiated the darkness, bringing all that was shrouded in shadow into sight. It sees itself from a more expanded perspective, and in the resultant lucidity, has the awareness – that it is the ALL.

*It is the Alpha and the Omega... the first and last, the beginning and the end.*

The *Cosmic I AM*, boundless and infinite, without end. In fact, a trinity – dark and light with a balance point in between.

From this illuminated space, it is able to extol and appreciate its dualistic nature; light and dark, good and evil, day and night. One not being better than the other, but there to allow the experience of the totality of its being. For it is only by rendezvousing with the night can it divine how magically dazzling the day is. Or by beholding the dark, can it appreciate the light.

Yet is this wee glimmer into its being; this nugget-size view, sufficient to quell its insatiable appetite to experience more of itself?

What if it were to individuate itself into many fractals? With each fractal containing a spark of this life force energy, thus providing a unique perspective... a new and titillating angle or view of itself.

It does so. Becoming like a multi-faceted crystal, with each facet emitting and reflecting the most beautiful light. Wherever the light crisscrossed, casting shadows to form a cascading crescendo of light and shadow. As again, it is all these parts.

It is the entire Universe expressing and experiencing itself in the most creative and imaginative way possible.

What imagination it has! It can be anything, anything that it imagines itself to be. It only needs to conceive it – and poof, it is manifested in the blink of an eye. The air, water, land and trees...every creature that creeps and crawls, walks or flies. It creates everything, as it is everything and it is also you.

You too are this fractal, a unique facet of Creation. Just as the leaves, flowers, fruit, stems branches and roots collectively make up the tree to which they are a part, you too are an individuation and part of the collective energy called God. Knowing this, where do you imagine your story began?

Do you imagine that it began at infancy or before that? Or perhaps – that you were sired from a daydream, created from the grandest vision that Creation ever had?

Because it is in all things, then you must be one of the things of which it is a part. As you are it and it is you, then you too must be a powerful Creator; a formless and infinite source of energy with the ability to create Universes, of which your current reality is just a part.

But wait a second. What do you mean by *I can create Universes?* If I can create Universes, how is it that I do not have the mental recollection of being able to do so? What sort of mental gymnastics ...jiggery-pokery balderdash is that?

Yes, it does boggle the mind, doesn't it? But did we not say to you to leave the mind at the door? But since you insisted on bringing it along...

What if you indeed had access to all the knowledge of the Universe, but prior to incarnating into this earth, you agreed to have – not all, but much of your memories under wraps? Existing as the ingrained knowledge that's the embodiment of your higher self, and electively doled out to you in blips and snippets, to aid you along your path.

And by path, I do not mean a well-laid out candlelit track adorned with all the bells and whistles to get you to where you imagine you need to end up. Or that there's one and-only-one hurdle-free route that's afoot. If this were the case, you'd likely be too caught up in the utopia of your experience to even pick up this book.

No. The path alluded to here is a different one. Not leading to any distinct destination or goal. It contains many detours and side turnings... many a twist and turn. In fact, there are a myriad of experiences, perfectly orchestrated to allow the exploration of select themes deemed relevant to this incarnation, that further shape and refine the soul.

In this way, there is no destination...no finish line. No piston sounding in the distance – *Ready... Set... Go...* No sudden dash and flurry of bodies worked up in a high-pitch frenzy, eyes focused with laser-like intent on some designated place ahead.

Nor relays to race. For it was never about the destination, and always about the process. It's a process that cycles back unto itself, with each iteration aiding a more magnanimous view of your continually expanding self.

In keeping, this book is not meant to proffer any earth-shattering conclusions about who you are. *Sage, Wizard, Godling or Manifestor,* though a powerful manifestor you undisputedly are. But rather to invite you on a journey of ecstatic self-discovery and remembrance. A journey back to yourself.

# 2

# Manifesting a Different Version of You

Knowing what you now know, can you begin to imagine how powerful you are?

If this fills your mind with thoughts of pulsing biceps, action heroes wearing capes cavorting off the roofs of sky-high towers, or executives in stilettos and Prada strutting with gilt-clad briefcases. Well yes and no.

Yes, in that you have the power to manifest, and I mean literally – manifest anything you desire. In the ensuing paragraphs I will give you a formula for exactly how. And no, as I'd like to invite you to explore a different definition of power than the one you may have been brainwashed into accepting, or initially conceived of.

You see; while having authority and influence over others may cause many to salivate and drool at the mouth, the truest definition of power is the level of control you exert over yourself. As, true power is not something you wield and flaunt to manipulate others, but rather – comes up under them like the wind, gentle and unseen, uplifting and empowering those around.

And while not be seen, it is most certainly felt...

In fact, if you were to harken back to the instances in your life when you felt most invincible, would you not agree that it was a feeling? You, speaking to a room full of people and seeing them completely riveted. Or perhaps, freewheeling through a set of twenty or so bench presses, having never picked up a barbell a single day in your life.

At the crux of which was the potency of the feeling kindled within. It's this very feeling that's at the heart of, and key to you becoming a powerful manifestor.

And whether manifesting consciously or unwittingly, it's the most potent ingredient there is.

Regardless of what you are conjuring or attempting to concoct, how you go about it, or denotation used – as many squabble over its name. *Witches may call it spells, pilgrims... prayer, and scientists.... quantum physics.* Nevertheless, I assure you, the formula remains unchanged.

It begins with an incantation, the speaking or spelling of that which you seek. As, you've likely heard that words are *Spells.* For it is in the speaking of it, that it is given. An entire Universe ready and waiting to orchestrate whatever musical notes are spelt. More so, when uttered in the throes of passion or gripped by a spell of rage.

It doesn't matter the modality used, whether written or spoken, or simply a thing that is thought. Each note or syllabus carries within it a particular frequency that is translated and interpreted by a Universe, that springs into action like an over-zealous child – keen and eager to play along.

Even so, in as much as words are spells... the feeling that evokes the words is the current; a wave that unapologetically sweeps up all in its path. Much like a relentless tornado, focused with laser-like intent on divining the most breathless reality from the vast ocean of possibilities, at hand.

The faster the eddy... the stronger the wave. Churning with breakneck speed to bring to shore and fruition, all that has been requested in the most exciting way imaginable. As the Universe – that is Creation, has quite the imagination, as shared.

In short, the feeling that's evoked by the thought, is the driving force and engine behind how quickly the Universe delivers. So, if that feeling is feeble and lackluster, let's say... the invocator lacks conviction, the witch is perhaps not feeling as magical, or the pilgrim is bereft of faith... what's already made manifest hovers in a space of limbo. The tide being too low and languid, hence keeping it at bay.

Many that call themselves witches and wizards, mages and sages, know this. Know not just to cast the spell, but to communicate with earnest, the gravity of what they desire – through the heart.

Yet with practice, may delude themselves into believing that they have been endowed with special powers that those around them that bear witness to this cosmic sorcery may also believe they have. And aptly so. For once you've gotten a taste of your own power, it can be quite a nostalgic ride, I dare add.

But are they delusional? Are these folks haplessly mad? Or have they somehow managed to tap into, whether primed to harness this mystical energy from childhood or chanced upon it later, that infinite reservoir of power that is our very birthright? That is also yours to access, if you so command.

If hearing this sends chills up your spine, perhaps it's the realization that you do not have to remain a passive bystander, allowing yourself to be hurled and hurtled mercilessly by the unsteady torrents of life. But can, starting now – grab the reins of your life, and reclaim the power that has been lying dormant all the while.

Just as well, you do not need a broomstick or any kind of *Ouija* board, though you can certainly frolic with such things. If doing so, further kindles and adds to the wave of elation, that even as you read these words, may be noticeable stirring within.

Pen, stencil, paintbrush, ink – you can pretty much use any implement you desire. Your life's a blank slate, and yours to draw, write or paint on it, as you like. In so doing, you get to harness your imagination, bringing each thought, each idea, or spell to life. Imagination is the language of your soul. So, let it run free... let it run wild.

Try this. Hold within your mind's eye a picture of that which you desire and add as much mental texture imaginable to it. Become the Picasso of your creation, imbuing it with a sense of playfulness and panache. Envision the shape, tone and color in as much detail as you can muster. The greater the detail, the more cogent the craft.

You are the artist. At any moment, can wipe the canvas clean. Or scrap the pages and create anew your story. Isn't this then, the most magical form of art?

Yet, the most brilliant creations are borne of a single idea, inspired by the imagination, and fueled by the heart. As the heart is the motherboard not the mind.

Nothing worthwhile ever arises from an endless stream of thinking; thought after thought falling over on themselves, jockeying to outperform the other and hold sway. Each one grander and more elaborate than the next. A convoluted mishmash of circuitry, completely cut off from the motherboard and disconnected from the main.

Though not broken, frayed or dismembered in any way. The connection is still there. Everything flows from and is connected to the heart; an invisible yet incessant stream of energy radiating out across space-time with each heartbeat, and every pulse.

Wave after wave of vibration, quantum entangled in an animated cosmic dance with all other hearts and synchronized to the universal pulse, requiring just a wee shift in perspective to tap back into this ecstatic flow. As that which warms the heart augments it, and constricts the heart staunches it, rendering the dance sloppy and slow.

Which brings us to the next vital step within this cosmic formula. Once the die has been cast, the spell spoken, and the feeling of enchantment evoked – it's necessary to sustain the feeling. And even more imperative to keep the faith.

Which is not to suggest an impetuous rampage, questing after every and all things that excite and elate. Though such adventures may well have their place.

But rather, to move unfailingly towards that which is within reach, and feels most thrilling in the moment. Also, ceding the usual dawdling and indecisiveness, graciously surrendering to the will of the cosmos and allowing the Universe to do the rest.

How your creation unfolds is irrelevant. Just as the trusting ballroom dancer allows herself to fall back into the expectant arms of her partner, that readily takes the lead and artfully maneuvers the dance. Once the spell is cast, the Universe is already at work, sculpting the masterpiece. Never leaving a single detail to chance.

In this way, your only job is to remain vibrationally synchronized to your adept partner, understanding that what you desire already hangs at the cornerstone of Creation. Ready to make manifest in your reality, if you'd just let it in.

For it's a very delicate dance. One misstep can muddle the gambol... thwart the outcome and completely derail the entire choreography, in the blink of an eye. So, trust the process, surrender to the mystery of what is being orchestrated, and embrace the changes and transformations that are set to flow in your life.

Though, if you imagined the Universe to be an unenterprising, predictable partner, you are in for quite the surprise. Why? Did you imagine that things would materialize quite in the manner you surmised?

# <u>3</u>

# *Embracing Change*

Steady now. If hearing that unexpectedly rocketed you into the zone of uncertainty. A warm welcome. You are exactly where you need to be.

I'm where I need to be? The mind ricochets with a million questions, a quick scan of the room affirming that which you already know. The clock ticking on the wall or its futuristic replica resting slavishly on your wrist – marks time. How long has it been? A week, a month... perhaps three?

But nothing has changed, the voice in your head bewails – at first softly, growing noticeably louder as the emotion of the experience floods back in. I've rolled the die, cast the spells, written in stone and sand.

The outcry is met by a deafening silence, the momentum of mixed expectations echoing off the walls. A mix of highs and lows...faith eclipsed by skepticism; a muddled cocktail of commands – the inconsistency of which leaves the Universe grasping to determine what it is you truly want.

Back and forth, back and forth...what a wearisome, wobbly dance.

Even so, the waltz must go on. Bodies intertwined and perfectly tuned, pantomiming a capricious dance. Almost on the verge of a climax; only to be derailed by a moment's hesitation, some trifling doubt.

As consistency is the key. You cannot ask the Universe for one thing and practice the vibration of the lack of it. It would be like an addled sailor navigating his dinghy every which way, oblivious to where the tide turns.

A positive tide draws the boat stacked full of that which you desire to you, while a negative tide pushes it out to sea. A relentless wave of possibilities – all skewed in the direction of your frequency.

Your vibration acting as a cosmic lighthouse, transmitting into the Universe an unseen yet powerful edict, as you can't disguise energy. You cannot fool the Universe. Not when energy; the unspoken language of the Universe, which you are continually emitting – is in every moment, loudly proclaiming how you are.

Moreover, how can you truly mask from that which is innately a part of you? The Universe is not external to you, but within. It's masterfully architected by your consciousness and projected outwards, to allow for the illusion of this physical experience. What a compelling mirage it indeed is.

This requires some annotation, so let's backpedal a bit...lets slow to a grind and unravel the threads of this intricate patchwork ever-so-gingerly.

You understand now that you are an integral part of the vast and exquisite tapestry of Creation; a soul having a human experience within this earthly realm, or so it may seem. And if you were to employ that unparalleled imagination of yours, you'd likely infer that upon birth, your soul by some otherworldly means inhabited your body.

While to a degree true, this is a rather simplistic and cursory postulation, providing only a tiny glimpse into the true nature of your reality. For the story of how you came to be on this earthly plane is a bit more impressive than that.

You see, your soul never in actuality leaves the spiritual, non-physical realm. It remains there, with a portion of your consciousness focused in such a way to create the illusion of the physical reality experience. Within the non-physical realm – yet imagining that it is not. It acts out the charade of momentarily forgetting itself, so as to experience and know itself from a different angle or stance.

In this way, the soul does not literally inhabit the body, as your soul is not within the body. It is your body that is within your soul.

While this may be hard to fathom, nothing materially exists outside of your consciousness. Everything you perceive within the physical world is simply a mimicry of your inner world, and a projection of what's occurring within.

It then stems to reason, that if you care to change what's showing up in your external experience, you must first create the change within. As the kingdom of heaven, the domain of your reign; a realm within which imagination dances to the titillating rhythm of your emotions to sculpt the façade of your reality is not without.

Reality, a façade? There goes that voice in your head again, grappling to connect the dots... unwittingly balking at the unfamiliar.

Oh, but the experience of physical reality is very much real; the elixir of feelings flowing unrestrainedly over a mosaic of interwoven moments. Not to mention the learnings – rooted in instances of profound clarity that tickle your senses and playfully tease open the doors of your perception, illuminating that which was formerly veiled. In fact, how you feel is what truly matters, as well as the ensuing expansion from insights gleaned.

Regardless of the type of experience or cast of characters you find yourself with, in every interaction – be it alone or with others, there is a discovery... a reflection or takeaway that graciously expands your consciousness. Each encounter is flawlessly designed and orchestrated to allow a fuller understanding of yourself.

In this way, every experience – albeit small, benefits you in some way, creating the changes upon which your external world is patterned and shaped.

In fact, each is a gesture of divine artistry, characterized by a breathless realism that animates your canvas with each brushstroke. Much like a master artisan, molding your reality with a dexterity that's beyond mortal grasp. With every inch of this exterior masterpiece, bearing the lasting mark of, and permanently altered by your touch.

Though the change may be so small, to where it's almost unnoticeable. Yet as your internal world ebbs and flows, your external reality must move in tandem with it. So, it isn't that there is no change. It's that, for change to be truly meaningful and enduring, it must start within.

Must take root in the cradle of your consciousness, and from there... cascade out.

As to seek on the outside that which you do not feel is to quest in vain. It's a hollow pursuit, bouncing aimlessly off the walls and forever echoing through the corridors of your mythical outer world. Eventually, it circles back unto itself and leads nowhere, destined to collapse under the weight of your misplaced expectations.

Or worse yet, you find yourself meandering around like an aimless wanderer, easily uprooted and adrift in the wind. Caught in the gust of your own delusions. Your ideas and desires never quite gaining traction... as they were never anchored to begin with or rooted in anything real.

You plough through the convoluted maze of your reality, only to uncover that all roads lead home... and all paths converge to the untapped oasis within. Home is where the heart is. As such, when you act from the heart space; when the very essence of the Universe mingles with the ethereal tendrils of your desires, an inner transformation occurs that sustains.

In transforming, you shift ever so slightly, ever so subtly to a dimension that is more in alignment with the new frequency that you are being. A parallel earth that's similar but not quite the same. If it looks different, it's because it is different. How can you change your frequency and still be in the very place you were previously in?

*Um, did I hear that correctly? Changing my frequency shifts me to a different earth?* The mind screeches to a halt. Eyes flit left to right; darting covertly around the room as if to assess the validity of what was just shared before the mind – once again into action, leapfrogs.

But everything looks the same. The wailing turns into a low, beseeching moan.

Yes, it's a stretch of the imagination to believe in the existence of that which you cannot see. Yet to comprehend this, you must understand that in going from one reality to another, the change is quite subtle and is often overlooked or missed.

So much so, one would readily shrug it off as a moment's DeJa'Vu.

Like you hastening to the kitchen to grab something and having no inkling of why the instant you're there. After a moment's faltering, what feels like a temporary bout of amnesia is pertly dismissed with a self-effacing chuckle. But is that really what it is?

Or was that momentary lapse of forgetfulness that left you mentally grasping for a memory that has long faded, the result of, the memory never being yours?

Belonging to a different version of you; one of the many versions of you that exist within a cosmically netted web of alternate universes, coexisting side by side.

An infinite number of earths rotating in concert with each other. Queued like a line of eager, agoggled spectators, watching and waiting with bated breath with the rest of the Universe to see if you'll make the leap – make the jump, towards them.

All it takes is a wee shift in your frequency, a slight change of your internal state to catapult you to a higher timeline. And send you spiraling through this universal lineup of proximate realities to a similar earth that is vibrating at a much higher frequency, than the one in which you're currently in.

Now, understanding that your internal state is constantly changing and in flux, do you still harbor qualms of remaining static, of being stuck? If so, shush your mind for a moment, and really allow this to sink in.

You cannot not change. In every moment you are transforming and evolving, whizzing through countless dimensions and timelines. This is, without question, the multi-dimensional nature of what you are.

Knowing this, all that remains is for you is to take charge of that which is readily within grasp – your vibration, the undulating rhythm of your frequency. By releasing all doubts, fears, and misplaced qualms that staunch the flow of your incessant desires, including the hang-ups of a fickled intellect, as doing so places you into the heart?

Do you know, when you master the art of navigating the world from the heart, it becomes a deliciously lighter place – much lighter indeed?

# 4

# Lightness of Being

*Light as in weightless, absent of that which has weight.*

*Light as in, that which illuminates. Revealing what was previously hidden and paving the way to clearly see.*

*Being as that which is effortless and unfolds in the space of no mind.*

*Being as the energy that is devoid of definition – as it simply is.*

Like a prismatic shaft of soft light radiating off the surface of a stream of water, allow these definitions to play a gentle staccato in your mind. Flitting playfully against the water's surface. Never disturbing the surface – light as a feather, essentially weightless, causing not a ripple to fall out of place.

The water glistens from the rapt attention, basking shamelessly in the light. Warmed by the tantalizing heat, penetrating and soothing its frigid depths. A clear and unwavering mirror, reflecting all the subtleties of this resplendent light; every color, every shade, every hue. Much like staring into the unjaded gaze of a newborn child.

In each place that the light caresses the water, an alluring pattern is formed. The diffused rays tattooing an ethereal array of light and shadows that appear to gyrate to some unbeknownst frequency, with the light and water – caught in the creative throes of a raw and unfiltered dance.

It's a movement that is felt at the deepest level, within the crests and valleys cloaked beneath the water's surface. No shadow can evade the gentle touch of this iridescent light that ripples in all directions, far and wide. There's no escape.

As light is its true nature... its true form. With the power to transmute any shadow, and like a master illusionist, to nimbly sidestep or maneuver unscathed through all within its path. Enticing onlookers with its bevy of antics; an evocative mix of shock and sensuality, the likes of which leaves the audience gasping for more.

The brilliance of the performance is shadowed by the enigmatic mystery of the mind-boggling stunts; a masterful interplay of shadow and light that captivates the imagination. Yet, both are essential; shadow and light – in this chimerical act. Each providing a needed contrast for the other. For, it's only from delving into the deepest, darkest abyss of our own shadows, can you truly appreciate your light.

When you find yourself in a space where there's nothing left to lose. As you've long lost sight of the attachments you thought mattered; the very ones that gulled you into thinking they were paramount to your existence. Until you yourself started to believe in this fallacious storytelling. That without the house, the job, and people who magically fell away – life would be intolerable.

It may have felt this way for a while. But then little by little, a lightness crept in to inhabit the space left behind by these fatuous things that had long departed. In the resultant lightness, you started to radiate with an undeniable brilliance. As in that moment, and the moments that followed, you had finally let the mask slip.

With no distractions competing for your attention, you finally turned the focus of your awareness on yourself. Coming face to face with the person staring back in the mirror that met your eye with a brutal honesty that belied the reality of one that bore rights to such a specious past. Forced to take a hard look at all the unspoken truths that nested in the shadowy realms of your being, that leapt and capered on the irradiated walls of your awareness, now that there was no one around to hijack your gaze.

I'm no stranger to this oh-so familiar tale.

I recall the first time I shaved my head. I was driven to a place where I deeply desired to rewrite my story – to tear up the pages and rescript the narrative, as the melodrama that had been playing out on my movie screen was a pretty, doleful one.

You know the kind; where the lines that delineate tragedy from comedy become blurred? And you find yourself manically laughing as if half-expecting the scene to precipitously change, or for some actor to wittingly pop up and expose the plot as the farce that it had been all along.

But no one shows up to rescue you, and no one will. Deep-down you knew this. Even as the laughter faded to obscurity in the almost deserted amphitheater of your mind, and you grimaced from the unfamiliar discomfort of sitting with yourself. As the mask was not just the kind that obscured others from seeing you, but one that hung precariously in the balance – obstructing your view of yourself.

So, you teeter back and forth, caught in a mental conundrum of your own making. Replaying every act, every scenario, every scene by memory; picking it apart with the eyes of a screenwriter... nipping and cutting the parts that were never savory to recreate the perfect pitch in your mind.

And as if this itself is not enough – putting ink to paper; feverishly scrawling as if the act of not commemorating this momentary clarity would be the undoing of your salvation. With every word... every syllable scribed, a defiant act of imposing reason on your intractable world.

Back then, I had made a list of all the old habits that were not anymore acceptable to me; the people-pleasing gimmicks acted out to elicit a smile, a word of complicity, a nod of approval. It was bottomless. The culmination from a prolonged period of not being myself and acting out a charade, perfectly scripted by my external world.

Even before the ink dried, the character painted leapt from the pages of my imagination, and the room crackled with an otherworldly energy – as a ray of hope crept in. It was time to doff the mask. Not tomorrow or the next, and not incrementally. Now!

I imagined a whole new movie playing out before my eyes, with a string of actors hitting all the old, familiar cues, all the practiced prompts. But it did not matter that they were, as what was different about this plot was that I had changed. The landscape was still the same, but the main character in the movie was now transformed.

It took a dark night of the soul, immersed in and forced to face my own shadows, and examining the beliefs that blossomed and were enacted out in the halls of my persona, to show me what I did not prefer. And less than a night; the span of a burning incense, to have clarity on what I did. There was no escape route... no detours. The only recourse on the well-laid out track of my resolve, was to change.

And change I did.

## 5

# A Bulletproof Plan

The first change I decided on was that I was going to tell the truth no matter what. By truth – I do not mean a tactless rampage to vent years of pent-up emotions and let loose the words that had been cramped down time and time again, that now jostled excitedly at the first whiff of freedom.

Nor was it an invitation to traverse down memory lane and set right, with past nemeses, the old scores and injustices long expired and forgotten.

It simply meant that I was never again going to consciously say things I didn't mean; utter words that didn't represent my truth and speak to dispel the awkward silence within a room simply to entertain another – ever again.

In each instance, I would let my words pass through three gates. *Is it true, is it necessary ... and is it kind?*

The key word here being *consciously*. As much like an untrained marksman, the expectation is not to hit the target on the first try. But to inch stealthily and steadily closer. Your marksmanship thence becoming niftier and impeccable with time. Through relentless practice, and by becoming the watcher of your words.

Do you know that the most powerful manner of speaking is with brevity, expending the least amount of energy – yet moving hearts with your words?

Words that have the power to uplift the heaviest of hearts, soothe the most skittish of minds, and nudge open the most walled-off of ears. For the heaviest words are the stones cast in judgment, and ones that float un-noticed past barred and bolted ears. There's nothing weightier than sharing your truth with another, that is not open and receptive to hear.

Expelled loftily – yet quickly faltering, as attention or the lack of it, has the momentum to create or dismantle worlds.

To topple that which is not any more desirable, like a sandcastle, artfully erected on sand. What you withdraw attention from rapidly fades. And it was time to redirect the focus of my gaze to the untended world within.

Which also meant never manipulating my external features and behaviors to soothe and appease the expectations of others. Having lost count of the numerous times I'd laughed and guffawed ... crowed and tittered at things I could not comprehend. While the mind worked overtime like a hackneyed laborer to decipher the incoherent mutterings of another, just so it made sense.

Time and time again, I contrived a smile. When my lips, gums and teeth had all banded together in protest of what felt unnatural, to relieve the leaden feeling of the obligation that weighed like a knapsack of rocks against my conscience.

All this, just to keep another within the room.

Even when it meant subduing the needs of my inner child that longed to express freely – its childlike wonder, as it's the only way it knew how to be.

Yet, my inner child was not the only one that was subjected to this harsh purgatory. The cells in my face, that were repeatedly schooled to appear relaxed when tired, elated when sad, calm when angry... especially when in a professional setting.

Time and place mattered, according to the stockpile of definitions and conditions that I had involuntarily imposed on myself.

That day, for the first time, I set all these definitions down. I allowed them to roll off of me like water on a freshly waxed automobile, and started to frisk and flirt with the notion of simply allowing myself to be, as I am.

No action was premeditated. None too much. There were no rules nor rubric, apart from the criterion to express with total abandon all which had been repressed before. And just like that, my inner child started to play again.

At first cagily, as if unsure of this newfound freedom, then exploding with unrestrained gusto. She had my uncensored approval, and there was no external rubber stamp … no one's assent – spoken or unspoken that was needed, but my own.

This did not mean evading or reproving the judgments or criticisms opined, or ballooning with unbridled pride in the wake of praises sung. But allowing them to wash over me dispassionately, as these external cues no longer held sway over my world.

And – what a world!

In this renewed universe, no one; person, group or entity was held above or below me. As those exalted that strutted with self-invented chips on their shoulders had been unceremoniously toppled from their podiums and made to stand on equal footing, regardless of creed or rank, while the downtrodden were lifted-up.

The master-servant dialectic was unreservedly shattered, which also extended to the notion of time. As in that instant, I'd also decided to die to the illusion of time… making it my servant. Not anymore allowing time to tow me back and forth as it liked.

Gulled into thinking it had control of my existence. Organizing and reorganizing my reality to fit in these neat, compartmental boxes that I was then tasked to shrink the expanse of presence into, thence yanking me unceremoniously out of the now.

This, however, did not mean abandoning the notion of time altogether. By no stretch of the imagination did I conceive a plane with its berth stuffed full of passengers to patiently dock awaiting my leisurely arrival. Or that I'd saunter into a roomful of clients only too thrilled to organize their schedules around mine. But using it sparingly, only when needed, and dropping this concept almost completely from my personal life.

With this, ended the rushing about – the mad hatter races with no finish line in sight, and making tons of plans, half of which I already knew I had no intention to keep. As at heart, I've always been a creature that rose and fell with the cycles of nature, that scampered not to the dictates of the conditioned world, but my own.

The more I stepped into the now, the anxiety, aches and undiagnosed ailments fell away, as the mind was not anymore caught in a vicious cycle of flight and fight. It was no longer throwing up all manner of safeguards to ensure its half-baked agenda went off without a hitch. In fact, without the insurmountable weight of the unrealistic expectations levied upon it, it finally simmered down.

Having grabbed hold of the harness of a once-fidgety mind, it seemed a natural succession that I'd make up my own mind about things, relying on my inner knowing. While simple sounding, this turned out to a quite a dodgy dance. It meant scaling back on the temptation to ask another what they think and evading the readily available stream of those – raring to unleash their esteemed opinions and meticulously doled-out wisdom on the world.

Yet the more I did that, the floodgates of my intuition were thrown wide open. The vast well of untapped Universal knowledge that had always been available to me, rushed in – sweeping me away with the force of an *Akashic* maelstrom, long suppressed.

In time, the invisible chains, taut from the tension of cleaving to a version of me long gone, fell away. Unshackled and free-footed, I stepped into pace with the beating of the cosmos. Before you know it, I was living in my highest truth and most authentic expression of who and what I am.

I now know that there is a direct correlation between the lightness of the soul and weightlessness of the physical being. For as the mind relaxed and released the needs and expectations of the conditioned world, my physical vessel followed suit.

My eyes came alight with an unmatched vibrance like embers of coals crackling with coveted warmth in the dead of winter. Smiles and laughter became effortless, as I was doing and being what felt natural, not because the world required it of me.

I had started to awaken.

# 6

# Awakening to the Dream

Boo!

Are you awake yet?

Or are you still swaddled within the lava-like folds of your blanket, savoring the nostalgic warmth of the old, familiar patterns; beliefs and doubts that hold sway to the lingering echoes of yesterday's past? You only need to open your eyes to dispel the shadows of their compelling mirage – to evade the grasp of this unseemly daydream.

Eyes surreptitiously closed flutter open, before shuttering again. Realization sets in, as this is not the kind of dream that requires eyes – not your physical ones anyway, though they've served you well enough. So, keep them shut or open at will.

Confusion etches neat little lines that furrow the brow, as if to mimic the jumbled folds of the spontaneously wrinkled blanket. But if not the physical eyes, then....? Words on the brink of being uttered trail off mid-sentence.

Somewhere within, there is a knowing, a remembering. A latent promise lying dormant. A promise to re-awaken to the truth of who you are; an inescapable truth that will flush clear the amnesia from your inner eye, allowing you to see through the carefully architected fallacy of this dream.

Every plot twist, and every turn. You realize, with a satirical twist, that you've been dreaming the entire time. That you've been making the whole thing up, imagining the entire story... masterfully concocting the entire plot.

You've imagined yourself asleep in nocturnal moments, under the swathing cover of the night, when in reality – this is the most awake you've ever been. When the mind ceases its relentless bicker, allowing the part of you that's your soul, to soar.

Soar it does. It reconnects to the astral realm to rollick in dimensions beyond the mundane perception. Thereupon, it re-merges with the whole of itself while still tethered to your slumbering body by the silver cord; an energetic tie that anchors and grounds the physical experience.

During this time, it's free to roam and frolic at will, relishing all which bolsters its expansion. Be it continued schooling in these realms or simply being a virtuous pillar to others. Whatever the agenda, be it healing, mentoring, seeking, exploring or aiding newly transitioned souls to cross over, hinges entirely on the mission of the soul.

It's an adventure that ensues as daylight breaks the dawn, when the body is to varying degrees rejuvenated and ready to re-enter the dream. It is ready to explore the uncharted halls of smoke and mirrors of this physical reality dream... this impelling mirage that will expand its experiential awareness immeasurably. As such, from the soul's perspective, it's all worth it. All of it... the entire *shebang*.

The illusion of pain, heartache, death, agony, isolation and separation; that we are separate from each other when we're not. Not to mention, all the other delusions that frame and decorate the halls and arcades of the seemingly mortal man.

Ghostly apparitions that parade wantonly down these halls, that haunt the alleys of your mind. Perceived as real only as you've forgotten your own immortality; blotted out the memory of who you are. The phantom of mortality looming larger than life – borne of an unsuspecting mind and deftly occluding this knowing. Now falling away like crusts from an amnesic eye.

Though you may not have known it then, all fear stems from the impending threat of loss or the death of a thing: loss of a prized relationship, reputation or life. An unpalatable list of probabilities – the unmaterialized imaginings of an egoic mind.

For death itself is illusory, in that nothing or no one literally dies. This includes your body; the smaller, visible portion of which disintegrates, while the larger energetic portion simply changes form. The latter being that which is impalpable to the naked eye.

It shapeshifts into a shimmering albeit invisible and energetically less-dense version of your former self and dematerializes, to pass unnoticed from this earthy realm. Millions of atoms flexing and gyrating in creative anarchy, delighted to break free from their physical prison, like an erratic wave of scintillating photons emitted from the plucked string of a guitar. From this heightened state, it remerges with *Source energy* – the non-physical part of you, at the end of the current life.

A single lifetime interwoven with other lives. Banded together like a string of precious pearls, and meticulously woven to form a closed circle that loops unrelentingly around the arm of the one that wears it. Well-fastened and steadfast, dare it gets lost.

Though nothing is ever truly lost, for why would Creation take from you that which is relevant to your experience? This can only mean one thing. That the elusive and at times coveted trappings that fell away; the very thing that you've been bemoaning, is not anymore needed in your experience.

By experience, I do not intimate that of the human persona that whines and whimpers at having to cede its attachments, but the divine part of you – the higher-self aspect that sees the whole picture within which your life unfolds. And how each scene, each meeting and person that comes and goes is tethered to your divine purpose.

It conceives the big picture, so you don't have to. So, you don't have to plan and plot every minute detail of your life. As such, it selflessly leaves you the time and space to cavort and play without worry, and to your heart's delight.

It knows that amidst all the playacting, you will at some point awaken from the subliminal dream and have the overwhelming curiosity to peek beyond the veil. The unshakable urge to unravel the mythical threads that weave the extraordinary narrative of your reality, allowing the most pristine view of who you are to emerge.

As the clearest mirror yet, is the vast Universe that sprawls and stretches in every direction around you – the people, plants, animals and other forms of earthly life. All divinely planted in your reality to reflect to you, the not-so-readily evident aspects of your persona that have craftily evaded your sight.

An entire Universe poised and ready to reveal to you the state of your consciousness; a string of loveless relationships mirroring your lack of self-love, or a joyless existence that reflects the feeling of melancholy within. Very quickly you see that when you smile, the mirror smiles in return. And when you love, it opens the floodgates for that love to return ten-fold, sweeping you impetuously off your feet, in turn.

You get a whiff of how supremely intelligent the Universe is. As without the gilded mirror that adorns the surface of your dresser, would you know what you look like? Can you say, without a sliver of doubt, that the person reflected – is you, and not some parallel reality version hovering somewhere in another dimension?

A hall of mirrors, reflecting to you, the many countless versions and realizable potentials of yourself. Mirroring not only those within your immediate and near reality, but in other parallel realms as well. All colluding in tandem across space-time, to animate the grandest, cosmic scheme, subliminally known to man.

The experiences of your life un-folding to the dictates of this monumental scheme: the ups and downs, wins and pitfalls, all befitting the themes you are to explore.

That's right – snags and challenges too, as you didn't reincarnate in this reality to experience a humdrum, pristine life. There's little growth in that. However, if you are operating from a place of conscious awareness, the experience can feel a seamless one.

When you stop invalidating the experiences encountered along the way by being more accepting to them and trusting that your higher self is leading the way. More so, when you surrender to the divine guidance received in each moment, even in this instance, as you are reading the words on this page.

Especially in this instant, and the many instances that will follow. As something has shifted within you. The energy that creates worlds has rocketed through you. The rose-colored glasses hitherto shuttering your view have slipped from their usual perch – and now that they're undoubtedly off, you tussle and squirm to put them back on.

You skirmish at the prospect of picking up where you left off, reassuming the same run-of-the-mill, lack-luster, cookie-cutter dream for the sake of not rocking the boat. Not wanting to unsettle the job and stability of those that depend on you; the spouse, geriatric parents and kids, even the odd coworker whom a few moons ago was unfamiliar – sacrificing your dreams for theirs. Or perhaps, never setting foot outside the borders of the reclusive town you grew up in, for fear of what lurks beyond the borders of your safe but judiciously buttoned-up world.

You get to the end of a timidly lived life, only to have the rueful realization that you've never permitted yourself to dream big enough. Forever swathed within the seemingly secure folds of your makeshift blanket, heeding the echoes of a dubious intellect.

But fret not, as there are countless opportunities to do it over again. This isn't your first and will not be your last reincarnation. Though why wait for another lifetime when the current one is at your fingertips? Are you daring enough to allow yourself to experience the grandest dream there is?

Are you bold enough to step unapologetically into the fullest and most expansive expression of who you are? To see the illusion for what it is, and lovingly sidestepping it. To skirt around those egoic hangups that give you pause; the feelings of obligation, shame, guilt and doubt – the mental and emotional weight of which was not yours to tug around anyway, though you somehow managed to convince yourself that it was.

Not allowing yourself to fall under the spellbinding clutches of the mind and the countless stories it tells. The mind is undoubtably one of the best storytellers there is. And such a tattle-teller! Have I shared with you yet – the beguiling story of the mind, and how bewitching it can be at times?

# 7

# The Storyteller Tells the Tale

Have you ever felt like there was a munchkin living in your head that just wouldn't shut up?

*Yappity...yap, Yappity yap!* An endless stream of yapping, like the deranged mutterings of a back-alley bedlam – except that it's coming from within.

It spews a barrage of oftentimes senseless babble, as if artfully wheedling you to partake in its abounding ramblings. Before you know it, you're deeply engrossed in a full-blown conversation with this imaginary prattler, out of touch with your present reality... out of touch with yourself.

With the only thing separating you from the loonies behind bars that dare to have these conversations out loud... is the lingering thread of self-awareness; that keeps you anchored to the whole of you. There's the knowing that the little voice inside your head is you, but not quite you. Yet, as you go about, you can't help but wonder about this talkative being, with the power and audacity to rattle your inner state.

As you are wondering about it, it's also wondering about you.

An innate intelligence that is very much a part of you, yet only a fraction of the divine being that you are. Though not cosmically engineered to think, or shoulder any of the number of roles imposed upon it by its habitually demanding human. Expected to play *therapist, analyst and shrink,* and lend an ear to the endless string of issues that bog down your oft times overly stimulated life. Not to mention the constant overthinking, jigsaws and mortal puzzlers. No wonder it breaks down.

In breaking down, it must then rebound – though rebounding with a different notion of what it's intended to be. It believes itself to be the problem solver, the riddle-buster and crutch of all your botherations, and that is has command of all your troubles. Moreover, it believes itself to have command of you.

Much in the same way as you've forgotten yourself, caught in a world of rushing about. Too busy parenting. Unfulfilled, yet brimming with the noise, clutter and distractions of the physical world. It follows that it too has forgotten how to be too.

That is, as an unseen companion that comes up under you as gently as a buoyant wind. It makes its presence known ever so subtly, yet keeping you anchored in this physical reality dream. With the intent to steer and usher you around this convoluted terrain. At the same time, translating the symbolic images and cryptic messages imparted by the higher self, in a manner most easy to comprehend.

Sort of like a mediator between you and the larger, non-physical part of yourself, and most effective when working in tandem with the whole of you – your higher mind, body and cells.

While the higher-self part of you divines the big picture – the entire landscape of forthcoming possibilities in your earthly mirage, the physical mind has a more focused view of things. As such, it is better able to assign meaning to what's occurring in the present or that which has occurred in the past.

To a degree, it's incapable of differentiating between what's transpiring externally and what's directly experienced by you. From the melodramatic film unfolding on the television to the dispirited lyrics of a melancholic song; filing these away in its storehouse of experiences, and taking everything observed – real or otherwise, as truth.

It draws upon this vast library of information, especially in the instances where the mind is unburdened and balanced, to shape, contour and give meaning to the universal guidance flowing through. For a balanced mind is fully receptive to this guidance, whereas an imbalanced one is not. Completely out-of-step with the higher mind, and in its quest for security, throwing up all kinds of defenses to secure its conceptual fortress, and sustain the power – it believes it has.

Like the perfect apprentice, feeling the surge of its dominance after years of continued training. Initially disgruntled by the weight of your taxing demands and expectations, but this soon fizzles, replaced by the familiar rhythm of its command. As once it has a taste of being in control, it will do anything not to relinquish its position.

It fusses and fumes within your headspace like a petulant child in the midst of throwing a fit. Habitually, spurting a deafening array of thoughts... the perfect antidote for anything that threatens its validity and balking at the mere hint of anything unsafe.

Yet much like a child you can coax and cajole it, recognizing that it's acting out from a place of seeking your validation. You can acknowledge its little antics, and gently but firmly guide it back to thoughts that are more in accord with who you know yourself to be – that feel more aligned and wholesome.

Just as you are a powerful manipulator, the mind is too. Quite the crafty trait, though not necessarily good or bad. In that it provides yet another mirror that plainly echoes when you are out of alignment, prattling and yakking incessantly when you are.

Seductive thoughts of a world that is out to get you, the villains that dishonored you or stifled your truth, and the ones that fail to validate you and show too little regard.

Before you know it, you are in a mental warzone erecting all kinds of boundaries, forts and defenses. As whether you realize it or not, you've fallen into the clutches of your ego rather than you having mastery of it... mind and ego being one and the same.

What the mind, however, doesn't know, is this little secret shared prior – that the world is a mirror, and your reality is a cosmic dream. Moreover, there are no villains lurking around the corner ready to inflict harm on you, unless of course, you created it.

With this knowing, you can now become the warden of your consciousness. Which is not to say, you are to vigilantly hound the mind... inundating it with your attention. As the whole point is to be outside the mind, not within it. But instead, notice the moments when it's rambling, plying you with less-than uplifting thoughts, and allow its stories to filter through these gates. Is it aligned – and if not, what is my underlying belief or opinion here. Moreover, is it true?

As shared, the mind is not very discerning. So, if what you're thinking is not aligned, simply choose to entertain a different thought. Bit by bit, as you resume control of the wheels and navigate your mental bogey in the right direction, the mind will give way and begin to quiet down.

For it knows well when to surrender, went to push your buttons and plunk your bells. And there are no buttons to push, when you are not anymore buying into the distorted stories it tells.

Nonetheless, we are storytellers by nature, so having an outlet to vent our imaginings is key. While as a child you were perhaps less inhibited about uttering these stories out loud, with time, you may have suppressed these creative musings. Or narrated them internally for fear of being denounced as whacky by a conditioned world.

Tucked well away and sealed. That which is meant to be shared unreservedly with others. The most magical expression of your soul and fertile expose of our passions under lock and key, when shackling this expression in anyway creates imbalance.

Shutters the heart, stifles the soul and rattles the countenance of an otherwise sound and agreeable mind. For even the mind hushes, becoming uncannily quiet when the heart comes alive, as if momentarily distracted and lulled under the spellbinding chorus of its rhythmically thumping sounds. As, how can anything clamorous exist in a space of chimerical bliss and resonant calm?

Imagination, as shared, is the unspoken language of the soul. And if you don't already have such an outlet; some exciting endeavor that allows your heart to soar, or creative pursuit through which you can surf the waves of your imagination – then how much longer will you abide in stifling the communion of your soul?

For you're always creating, always storytelling. This way of spinning tales, be it with your limbs, voice, or not-so-uncommonly a-rat-tat-tattling in your head, is in your nature. So, you cannot not tell stories, you just need to become more mindful of the stories you do tell.

This the case, wouldn't you rather tune in to the enlivening stories of your inner being, as opposed to the noisy ramblings of ear-splitting prattler that lives rent-free in your head?

# <u>8</u>

# *The Art of Silence, Tuning In*

Not all stories require words. The best one's hover in the spaces where no words are needed – or rather, where no words can be found.

Too many words... too many utterings, a smattering of non-unifying sounds. Meaningless gabber that shatters the stillness. What are words anyway, if not a crude substitute for a mythical albeit all-but-forgotten telepathic artform?

In fact, there's much that's shrouded within the silence – as silence itself, happens to be a rather poignant sound. Yet to truly hear it, one must first curb the erratic ramblings of the tongue.

Curb the tongue and cede to the ensuing stillness, becoming soft and pliable, to then dance to the noiseless echoes of a soulful drum. Moreover, subdue the stimuli assailing each of your senses, and tune each – much like the finnicky, over-stimulated strings of a violin, to where they're unknowingly plunking in unison.

For you yourself are a matchless instrument, carrying a signature frequency that is uniquely yours. Like any instrument that is repeatedly neglected, you too may grow dull and boorish, and off-key with misuse. Too busy tuning to those around you, rather than to the untapped symphony within. Too filled up with the external noise to hear the promptings of your inner being, to heed the voice of God.

A thump, a soft shrill... the constant ringing in the ear, initially quite subtle and becoming more impassioned in time. As the Universe has a guileful way of grabbing your attention, inviting you to slow down.

I say God – but again, call it what you will. The inner force that beckons you to that oh-familiar ring.

Something about the silence that lures you, something about the stillness that invites you in.

So, you pause for a moment savoring this melodic calm, while each of your limbs, unused to this slavish passivity, protests at will. They itch and squirm and make a fuss, as while it may sound simple to submit to this momentary serenity, many come to realize – it is not.

Some age-old monks and *Bodhisattvas* know this well, same tucked away in solitary pursuit in a heroic bid to curtail the provocations of the heady world in which they dwell. Though what's suggested here is far less severe; a deceptively simple practice that will catapult you to new heights without undue trial or strain.

No reclusive exploits or off-grid feats, nor prolonged bouts of fasting steeped in stoic practices and punctuated by the cessation of speech. No efforts to quell the senses and nip unchaste urges in the bud, or ceding of things material less the ego runs amok.

Yet mastering this state does have its share of demands, requiring a high degree of self-awareness, commitment and command – taking care to tune only to that which nourishes you, and safeguarding against that which does not.

Which is not to feud and skirmish with those that disrupt your peace; an outcry of war, a spate of unbridled anger ... the inward stirrings of protest. Yet nonetheless, a call to action to subdue the noise at all levels of your being. And do so gently, as the art of silence is undoubtedly rooted in the mystifying blend of softness and finesse.

Simply put – it's the curbing of all that is extravagant and excessive, by tackling obesity in all forms. As well as a staunch resolve to anchor to the reposeful calm within you, rather than to the temperamental misgivings of an inherently fickled world.

If your mind balks at the notion of being obese, haggling and inwardly lamenting at the prospect of being called fat, understand that overweight in this context refers more to the aspects of your persona that are taxing. Those things for which you unnecessarily expend energy, and that which weighs you down.

Even so, there isn't a tried and proven list of dos and don'ts or cookie-cutter solution to share, as each person is different and there's never a one size shoe that fits all. Nonetheless, once attuned to the silence, it's impossible not to notice the discord. For all that's noisy and tips the balance springs into focus. It forces you to take notice, besieging you with a flurry of not-so-subtle cues to reorient you into harmonious accord.

So, as you traverse this world, are your movements lithe and calm? Or do you trudge around sluggishly, making unnecessary movements – perhaps caught in the throes of doom scrolling on your venerated gadgets or some other meaningless norm?

When you do act, is there a degree of presence to what unfolds? Do you ever pause to notice how your body feels, allowing these bodily sensations to guide you, or are you too busy scampering to the unreasonable dictates of your external world?

And I know well how demanding and distracting the world can be ... yet allow me to impart a little-known secret. Your body has a consciousness – an innate intelligence that expands and soars, the more awareness you bring to it.

It shrieks and squeals like a herd of banshees to get your attention – signaling when to scamper about and take action, and when to simmer down and relax. Moreover, it rails with the vigor of a newborn when the food you consume is replete with GMOs and toxins that spur your cells into overdrive. In so doing, rousing them to perform biotic backflips and somersaults in earnest, just to restore the balance.

For your diet should be mostly alkaline, comprising of fruits, vegetables, minerals and the right amount of protein to sustain robust cellular function. Straying clear of sugars and processed foods, as there's no better recipe for cellular malfunction.

When your cells and organs are working overtime, whilst you may not hear it, this too is a form of internal noise. Groaning and growling and puffing up gas, after a long spell of exhaustion ... to where they're almost hovering on the verge of collapse.

Once the body is noisy, the mind soon catches on, like an internal dialogue raging like wildfire throughout. Nothing can insulate from the crackling inferno of an imbalanced vessel, with every aspect of your being itching to chime in the conversation.

Yet again, the key to attuning the mind, is to pump the brakes and slow it down, and curb its tendency to meander by gently refocusing it. To where it's like a passive bystander, quietly wallowing and soaking in the surrounding sights and sounds.

Not having too many thoughts or opinions, as these take us out of the heart. They hinder our ability to feel, when emotions – be they agreeable or otherwise, are like telltale signposts, revealing to us when we're in alignment and when we're not.

Even so, all emotions heedless of their nature play a positive role. With imbalance arising, not by virtue of having them, but by regarding them as that which they're not.

To feel is so very vital, though the only true emotion in existence is love. With all other emotions, be it hate, fear or anger – simply outcroppings of the ego's reaction to an unfavorable event that doesn't placate its unsatiable need for security and love.

It wallows in fear at any looming change that may strip its sense of security, that causes your heart to patter fitfully, though this fictious event is unlikely to occur. And puffs up with pride and anger, when its esteemed honor or that which it deems invaluable is unceremoniously trampled upon, irreparably wounded or rebuffed.

Yet is your life really threatened, and was anything permanently lost? So rather than give in to the whimperings of a crotchety ego, you can simply notice when these secondary emotions crop up. See them as the teachers they are, and view them dispassionately, as then their formidable grip will eventually diminish and disperse.

In sum, physical noise dissipates when the body is still, mental noise when the mind is silent, and emotional noise when we are heart-centered and operating from a space of unconditional love. And there's an inner tranquility that is felt when all is in melodic accord, and the Universe spontaneously mirrors this harmonious state without.

It's a state that naturally manifests when you are doing less, focusing your gaze upon the present moment, and conserving your energy and words. More so, when you allow the echoes beneath the clamor to soothe you, and an expression of silence in all that you are.

Though it may take some getting used to, as it's no simple feat to set aside the ingrained habits of the past. Yet with practice and persistence, that which is innately natural will become second nature – illuminating to you the single, most powerful yet underrated practice. Why? Did you imagine I'd spill the beans and simply blurt out what?

# 9

# The Gift of Being

By being authentic!

*Being authentic? That's it!?* A faint flame of curiosity continued to flicker, almost as if in defiance of the encroaching wave of disappointment that threatened to rush in.

But there must be more; some catch twist, some unimaginable truth tucked out of sight – ready and raring to spring into view. Some earth-shattering proclamation aching to be revealed, with the possibility of expanding my consciousness leaps and bounds.

A noticeable whiff of disbelief and impatience punctuates the ensuing silence. With no further utterances' forthcoming, realization dawns that there may not be more to the simple, yet potent formula shared.

Even so, the mind steps into overdrive, churning the word *authentic* every which way, as if to unearth some hidden meaning within the word.

Yet it is as simple as it sounds. No bells or whistles, nor cryptic messages waiting to be debunked. No complex mystery to be unscrambled, nor mind-boggling codes and puzzlers, tucked out of sight from prying eyes – in the off chance of being cracked.

Nonetheless you're not completely off kilter, as the very notion of expanding your consciousness means that you are on the right track. And there's no faster way to do so than to express fully – your authentic nature. For what is consciousness anyway, if not the ever-increasing awareness and experiential knowing of what you naturally are?

Though increasing not in size nor brawn. Creation never expands structurally, only experientially. Which at first blush may seem rather limiting but happens to be the most awe-inspiring part. In that, nothing can augment, snag or rip asunder the threads of this one-of-a-kind tapestry of existence, of which you are an integral part.

No souls can be newly created, nor existing souls be made extinct. Moreover, no aspect of this exquisite tapestry can be replicated or altered – including you, without the entire structure unravelling and falling apart.

If you're frothing with astonishment at how very vital to existence you are, know that the very fact that you are part of this fabric means that you are rare and unmatched.

Not to be judged, diminished or pitted against another, who by their very essence is dissimilar to you. Free of the need to shrink or alter yourself to fit another's ideals or bigoted definitions of what you should or shouldn't be or do.

Why should you? When you've been created in the grandest image ever conceived. Your face and body perfectly shaped and sculpted by your higher self who has a panoramic knowing of every tryst and trial that is essential to its evolution and is intentional, with every line and contour... each freckle and blemish weaved.

Regardless of whether you find yourself lacking, perhaps constrained in a physical vessel that has been stymied and maimed. Yet even in this instance, there is a higher pretext; a specific experience being sought that transcends your lamentable circumstance – some unexplained reason that's part of a larger plan, though you may not readily grasp its meaning.

Perhaps your mission is to rise above your challenge and be a source of inspiration for the pocket of souls that share in your strait. But how can you achieve this, if you're off in a corner, sulking and moping? Or worse yet, manipulating your truth, expression and very essence, just to fit in and assimilate.

Thinking yourself easy to get on with by attempting to blend in with the world. When the best gift that you can give to anyone, is not the well-coiffured guise or tiring charade, but that of your authentic self. Completely removing the mask so others can see you, and decide only upon having this clarity, if they feel an affinity for what you are.

While you may win their affection and chance that they profess their love, in the instances that you're not being yourself, were they to swoon in your presence, is the person that they fell for – really you?

Not to mention the sheer effort to sustain the illusion. As heaven forbid, they had a glimmer of that which they shouldn't see; a scar, a blemish, a shameful truth tucked away in your mendacious closet. And departed, their perception of you forever scathed. Wouldn't you rather be rejected based on who you truly are?

If the prospect of shedding the façade scares you stiff, understand that people can only meet you to the depths to which you've met yourself. They provide the clearest reflection – a connection steeped in integrity, only when you yourself are truthful. For when you smile, the mirror always smiles back.

Hence, before you can be true to another, you must first shine the light of truth on yourself. By taking the time to unroot and unravel all the conditioned programs and superficial threads that bind you, so as to break free from the shackles of pretense.

If the perception that you're not beautiful or worthy enough gives you pause, it's time to shush the inner critic plying you with seething tales of ridicule and shame. Of the countless people lined up to judge you – if you don't submit to playing by the rules of their foppish societal game.

Your instincts spurring you to break away from conformity, the unquestioning compliance to ways that no longer serve you and herd mindset that's slowly deflated you from within. Until bit by bit, you erect a fortress around you, losing who you are under the weight of its hefty walls, as self-deception is rather a heavy burden to sustain.

Well-tucked away under the cloak of duplicity, emerging bashfully only when no one's watching; an ad-lib whirl, stealthy dance in the bathroom mirror or covert jig – quickly donning the mask the minute someone enters in.

Yet who are these people casting judgments, the very ones you believe care? When in actuality, no one's really paying close attention. Too caught up in the upkeep of their fragile existence, putting on acts of their own and tending to their personal affairs.

They pause to stare only when they spot something authentic, as what a rare and refreshing sight it is! A sight that stirs something deep within them. Your expressive vibe – an anthem of freedom and unapologetic living, beckoning at them to join in. For there is nothing quite as mesmerizing as one that's comfortable in their own skin.

Yet there are those that may initially despise you, your presence serving as a reminder of their own disempowered stance. Ready to balk at anything discomfiting; their desire for self-preservation overriding any discernment they may otherwise have.

Clueless to the real threat, the imposter that has usurped their sovereignty; a stealthy character and one of the many personas flaunted, that has craftily taken charge. While their true self lurks beneath the shadows, bearing witness to the unending string of feigned acts. It impassively watches as they unknowingly squander this one-of-a-kind earthly experience, too immersed in what others think and appeasing the world at large.

Unable to glean beyond the surface, as true discernment requires the knack to innately see. How then can you reasonably expect them to see you, when they lack the clarity to see themselves? So, adept at masking, they've long forgotten how to be.

It's rather a dodgy dance to attempt to control the uncontrollable, including the lens via which you're perceived. Not to mention, it was never your job to get others to like or see you, let alone fret and distress over how you are received.

Truth is – there's nothing that you need to disguise to fit in. As if the shoe doesn't fit, it's simply ill-fitted and out of place. In the same way, you cannot fit a square peg within a circle, you have no business shrinking yourself to fit any mis-aligned space.

You see – being the self is not about seeking alignment with others, but with the larger, divine part of you, and remaining steadfast in your truth regardless of how the world reacts. It's the ceding of all resistance, including the fickled cares and perceptions of others, and bringing the focus back to you.

Yet, it's never too late to bare the mask, as there's no one tracking your progress or keeping score. Moreover, the act of being the self is neither a destination nor a goal.

What it is – is an ecstatic journey, one of introspection, exploration and zest. With each experience inching you closer to a more profound realization of yourself.

As there's a special intimacy that's felt by those in alignment with themselves. Yet how can you come to know this feeling, if who you are being – is someone else?

# 10

# *Intimacy — Into Me I See*
## *Understanding the Rainbow Body*

*I always felt butterflies are like flowers with
wings.
The type of flower that continually sheds its
petals...
Only to reveal new, softer, more delicate layers
within.*

In some unbeknownst corner of the world, a pupa
sits in hibernation swathed within the folds of its
cocoon. In rapt stupor – you'd think? Or perhaps, this
may well be a phase of deep introspection. A natural
turning inward to really know and understand itself,

and thereupon, share the newly realized version of itself with the world.

Eventually, it emerged from its nest, completely transformed. It unfurls its wings to reveal the most breathtaking sight; the majestic, winged creature that it has become. But only upon shedding the superfluous aspects of itself that are no longer needed, becoming light and unfettered, to thenceforth soar with ease into the light.

Yet if a kind passerby was to attempt to free it from its impregnable abode, before it had the chance to wiggle its way into freedom, would its spindly legs be nimble enough to balance? Would its wings be strong enough to soar?

You know the type; the charitable doo-good-er that gets a high from fixing-up others and saving them from themselves, regardless of whether the aide is needed, or rendered in a way that truly helps.

Sometimes the most beneficial thing you can do is to allow nature to unfold at its own pace, as opposed to prematurely stepping in. Giving yourself grace and space, being that you too are an extension of nature, to tap into the divinity within.

Seeing the so-called hermit mode, not as a phase of social seclusion, though seemingly self-imposed, but as a blessing in disguise. With the Universe shrewdly propelling you inwards, much like the butterfly – to uncover more of who you are and rediscover yourself with new eyes.

It's the way that your inner being beckons to you when you've wandered off the path. How it invites you to step away from the noise and return into your chrysalis where it's nice and quiet. So, you can better hear its promptings – better heed its voice.

And in these instances, you may well sense that something is off, as while you may feel the compulsion to plough onwards, your heart is giving you pause. So, you withdraw momentarily from the world, seemingly crestfallen and depressed. Though what this is, is a natural turning inwards – an instinctual returning to the self.

Still, you can't remain perpetually in hermit mode, wrapped up in your chrysalis, 'til ad infinitum. There comes a time after all the soul searching, when you must muster the courage to break out of your cocoon... and continue on.

Move on, and apply the insights gleaned from this phase of uncoerced solitude, to define yourself from a new perspective – a different point of view. For much like the butterfly, you too are evolving, and in every instant recreating yourself anew.

Spreading your wings to unleash your power and display your colors to the world. What if I were to tell you, that you too are beyond splendid – containing within your auric body... all the colors of the rainbow, though it may not be readily observed?

Though some can see it, and you may as well in time. As, when you're in complete alignment, these colors are quite vibrant, radiating outwards with such intensity, causing the entire rainbow body to come online.

Yet there's a way to train the peripheral vision to see another's aura, by strengthening the rods in the corners of your eyes. And if a wee bit curious, a basic rundown of your body's energetic centers or chakras in the ensuing paragraphs will help. An overview, that will come in handy as you sift through these pages, to expand the extra=sensory perception you have of yourself.

The 1st chakra also known as the root or earth chakra is represented by the color red and located at the base of the spine. It's concerned with all things' security, as well as your need to be safe and survive. To clear this center, you need only to release the fear-based beliefs that you've diligently acquired over the course of your iffy life, recognizing that all fear stems from the unknown. It's the ego's resistance to change, and the instant you make change your friend, these irrational emotions will fall away and subside.

When balanced, you feel grounded and rooted within. And may rest confidently in the knowing that you're well-anchored, like a tree with deep roots – unshakable and settled. Yet imbalances in this chakra may manifest as feeling lost or unsafe. Though nothing that a bit of grounding, walking bare feet on the earth, cannot remedy and fix.

The 2nd chakra also known as the sacral or water chakra, is represented by the color orange and located below your navel string. It's the center for creativity and sexual energy, and seat of all things addictive and indulgent. To clear this energetic center, you need just relinquish the guilt trips and inane quest to be perfect all the time. Guilt is simply the outcropping of a less than stellar self-image. It's perfectly normal, not to mention human, to make an utter and complete mess of things from time to time.

When balanced, you feel expressive – keen to harness your creative passions and gifts. Yet imbalances within this center may show up as co-dependency and cravings, a lack of creativity and bliss. The perfect antidote to which, is simply to reconnect with your inner child. Before you know it, you'll be romping about like an athlete on steroids, feeling energized and more enlivened than you've been in a while.

The 3rd chakra also known as the solar plexus or fire chakra is represented by the color yellow and referred to as the seat of the soul. It's located above the navel – the epicenter of your power and radiates when you're feeling surefooted and bold. To clear this center, simply desist from externalizing your power, ensuring to release all shame and self-doubt. As doing so allows your assertive, power-filled nature to emanate out.

While imbalances within this center may show up as low esteem and self-worth. The very fact that you're reading this book means you're a step closer to eclipsing these limiting themes and adopting a more wholesome narrative of your worth.

The 4th chakra also known as the heart or air chakra is represented by the color green and located in the midst of your chest. It's symbolic of your connection with your soul – being the oasis of compassion, love and zest. It's clogged by grief, loss and traumatic events that render you cynical and closed. Yet to clear this center, you simply need to see the lesson in each experience. For even the ones that drive you silly serve a higher purpose – inching you steadily closer to satisfying the agenda of your soul.

While imbalances within this center may manifest as apathy and distrust... understand that hurt people hurt people. Plus, the very act of loving yourself will foster a more compassionate view of antics you don't prefer. Yet, if there's ever an instant where you feel aggrieved or upset, a quick trip into nature may provide a much-needed reset.

The 5th chakra also known as the throat or ether 'space' chakra is represented by the color blue and located within your throat. It's the gateway for communication and self-expression and when balanced, you may exude a quiet confidence and candor when engaging with others, intimating your authentic self – in thought, deed and word.

To clear this center, you need only release that which is misaligned with your truth. For when blocked, communication may be repressed or difficult, leading to undue prattling or issue speaking up. Nonetheless, if you ever feel tongue-tied or constrained, the simple act of chanting 'Om' may do wonders and have you flowing again.

The 6th chakra also known as the 3rd eye chakra or pineal gland is represented by the color indigo and located at the center of your forehead. It's the seat of your intuition and gateway to the non-physical realms – the knowing of which may demystify accounts of lucid dreaming or other such psychic phenomena you might have had.

When balanced, you may experience great clarity with the knack to peer beyond the veil. And while imbalances may manifest as feelings of rigidity and lack of focus, you'll find mediation and a dash of natural light to be most effective at releasing the skepticism and self-doubt. It will evoke within you renewed insight and purpose.

The final or seventh chakra also known as the crown chakra is represented by the color purple and located at the top of your head. It's the seat of enlightenment and connection with your higher mind. When balanced, it may manifest as heightened awareness, inner peace and interconnectedness with all things.

While imbalances may have you feeling like you're in the midst of an existential crisis; disconnected, mentally fatigued and lost. To clear this center, you need only release the attachments that have you bogged down to the physical. Though a bit of yoga and breathwork practice may be remarkably effective in lightening you up.

When all chakras are cleared, rotating and aligned, it creates a pathway for the higher energies to travel up and down your spine. It activates the two kundalini serpents, now resting dormant at the base of your spine, allowing these energies to rise up your channel and merge, to form a union most divine.

The very act of this reunification is a transcendent experience that allows the experience of the Christed self. With Christed, simply being an allegory for the attainment of a higher, more ascendent state of consciousness.

This divine activation is set to occur when you're best positioned to handle this energy and merge with your godhead. As doing so, catapults you so much closer, into a place of true alignment and oneness with your highest self.

Fully integrated with the whole of who you are, and what a magical transformation it indeed is? Poised to become the cosmic, emboldened butterfly you are meant to be. Though now that you have a taste of your innate magic, how about you grab a pair of binoculars – and no, I do not mean that literally. But do come along with me, if the prospect of viewing your Universe from a more expansive perspective thrills.

## *11*

# *Bird's Eye View of Creation*

Eyes initially downcast, glance inadvertently upwards as if in anticipation of witnessing something transcendental above. But what's to see outside of you? Do you not know – your entire Universe resides within you? So, there's nothing of material consequence external to you, to be particularly mindful of.

Every inch of it; every nook and cranny, tucked-out-of-sight corner, realm and dimension hovering patiently in wait, ready for you to tap in.

With each untapped dimension, leading up to the next, charting the way for your ascension. An inward path that leads you back to yourself. And before you get all gung-ho and tactical, remember it's never about the destination or goal. No finite rungs on the ladder for you to leapfrog over, nor contending levels to surmount or soar.

For in as much as you are a limitless energy with no beginning, middle or end, so too is the world around you – including your Universe. It contains within it an endless array of dimensions; a fraction of which are experientially relevant to the lifetime and version of earth you're currently in.

There are indeed an infinite number of dimensions above and below the earth plane, spanning further than your physical eyes can see and comprehend.

Notwithstanding,

*The process of Creation down through the dimensions is one of fragmentation.*

*The process of Ascension up through these dimensions is one of assimilation.*

One level being not better nor worse than the other, but comparatively lighter or denser, providing a much-needed contrast to evolve the understanding of your greater self.

And you're presently in a 4th dimensional Universe; three dimensions of space and one of time, progressively shifting and ascending into a realm of higher frequency, which is the justification for the current shift.

An entire planet awakening from a deep, amnesic slumber to rediscover the truth of who they are. Being not just a cloister of souls having a human experience, but vastly more nuanced and ineffably more than just their physical avatars.

This very awareness propelling them out of the pre-existing density and inching them closer to the light. As the further we advance in consciousness as a species, the more that's veiled dimensionally and subconsciously opens up, and trickles into sight.

This includes the veiled and shrouded aspects of yourself that were hitherto hidden, and in the dark. A most momentous occurrence. As you, like so many on your planet, endeavor to heal and reintegrate the fragmented aspects of your being, so as to fully experience the wholeness --- holiness of who you are.

If you've made it to this point, you'd know that Creation, of which you are a part is ubiquitous and by and large a paradox. In that, it expresses qualities that may oft seem conflicting; being up and down, right and left, everything and concurrently nothing.

In its undifferentiated state it is dimensionless – being a singular energy we call *The One*. It chooses to differentiate itself to know and better understand its own nature, as it's much more adept at beholding itself in its differentiated form.

This differentiated form of Source energy, God, *Yahweh* or however you refer to it exists in the uppermost dimension of Creation. It's the purest form of unconditional love and light. Which is why so many upon transitioning to the non-physical realm... presuming to have flitted through death's door, describe their re-mergence with this energy as most transcendental, being of unparalleled bliss and delight.

It's the tree of life itself – stretching its limbs to span the dimensions that are uppermost, with its roots extending to the realms below. Yet regardless of how low or high it reaches, know that every part of the tree constitutes the whole. Its branches willfully lighter, as intended to bear that which has less weight. With its roots in contrast being more sturdy, aka more physical, meant to charter unknown territories and straits.

In this way, Creation expands itself by fractalizing down though the dimensions, though again not structurally but by expanding its experiential knowing of itself. With each dimension containing extensions of this singular energy, and each proffering the perfect mirror that offers a unique glimpse of its nuanced and multi-faceted self.

The higher the dimension, the stronger the reflection or expression of this energy is. As think of it this way. If you were to hold a mirror farther away from view, how much of your own reflection will you be able to visibly glimpse?

Your reflection will likely grow more distorted, the farther away the mirror is. Though not necessarily darker, just more obscured by the shadows, which is not very different to how Creation operates. It becomes increasingly denser, the more it meanders down through the dimensions. Yet nevertheless, the relative density of the dimensions does nothing to subtract from the awe-inspiring beauty, that every aspect of Source energy naturally is.

In this way, the very 1st level of fragmentation, that which you may call the Celestial realm or dimension, provides the truest and clearest view. With the angels and Archangels holding the highest possible vibration, an energy imbued with light and love, and beaming this unremittingly back to you.

While a detailed account of the dimensions is beyond the scope of this text, it would be remiss not to touch upon the oversoul, hovering in a dimension much above our realm. These collective energies, as there are quite a few – believed to be approximately 600,000 in number, further fractalize to become the individuated soul that is me and you.

All souls incarnated on this planet are each an extension of an oversoul. With every incarnation, further spurring the expansion of Creation, through the experiential exploration of specific themes deemed relevant for the growth of each respective soul.

You may have had a life as a plant, animal or other being in another realm besides the earth. Though it may appear that these lives are separate, they are unfolding in parallel. For time is simply an illusion of our 4th dimensional world.

A bit above the 5th dimension is the realm within which the expression of the soul takes form. In the case of the earth plane, as you well know, this expression is a physical one. I say expression – as the soul literally remains in the non-physical realm. So, what you see is a mere illusion, created by your soul projecting a fraction of its consciousness into the physical reality dream.

This way, the higher-self aspect can maintain the big picture and not lose sight of its goal. All the while, distilling guidance to you in the form of intuition, messages, visions and synchronicities which happens to be its typical communication mode.

It transmits this information to your physical or egoic mind... same that keeps you anchored in the earthly dream. Else you'll be bopping around like a space cadet, way too unfocussed and unhinged, to satisfy the exploration of the agreed-upon themes.

Even so, among the many hats it wears – this is not the only role of the mind. It also acts like a recorder to archive away the many experiences amassed within your life. Accounts that are imprinted unto your spirit and later transmitted to the oversoul, adding to the ever-growing akashic records, brimming with all the learnings realized.

Yet regardless of the dimension you may have experienced or find yourself in, it's undoubtedly a special time to be on this planet to bear witness to the ongoing shift. For a collection of souls to have descended so far into the shadows and reemerge into the light – is truly a remarkable feat requiring mastery and prowess, if not a literal gift.

Even so, your outer world cannot evolve and shift unless the change is birthed within. Though change, it certainly will. As each vibrational shift at the individual level creates a ripple effect that's felt across the entire cosmos, affecting all there is.

From this broader perspective, allow yourself to soar to new heights. Habitually accessing your inner world to transmute all – veiled in the shadows, with your light.

Doing so, not to invalidate any aspects deemed crude or unsavory within yourself, let alone another – as relationships are key. With those closest to you, acting as the perfect mirror, illuminating these less than palatable aspects for you to see.

Tell me! Doesn't knowing this render you more curious towards others, to a degree?

# <u>12</u>

# *The Relation Ship*

Zoom in a little! Now, do you see?

Remember, you are the dreamer, and as such – it is your dream. Everyone around you, drifting about like tiny tots within your Universe, moving in perfect rhythm within your story... gyrating in seamless tandem to your tune.

Why? Did you imagine that they are real?

They look real, feel, smell and in a few surreptitious instances, even taste real. So why wouldn't they be?

Moreover, did you imagine them to literally be in your Universe? And would it startle you to learn that much like your reality, they too are holographic projections –extensions of your own energy, there to provide a rich context for this unfolding dream?

All the while reflecting to you with perfect clarity, the aspects of your own being, or rather manner of being, that you need to see. Frowning in unison with you, and loving most ardently, in the heady instances when you echo this feeling too. For the one that is loved becomes the lover, while the one despised may grow apathetic and aloof. Though not necessarily mirroring your action, but more aptly your frequency, reflecting to you in synchronous accord, exactly how it is you feel.

Each interaction is an orgasmic explosion of co-creation, with every character responding to the oscillating frequency of your script. While the themes of your story may well be predetermined, how the script unfolds is truly at your discretion. As if every detail was perfectly architected, how then would you define free-will?

A cast of revolving characters lined up and waiting to step into your play. Into parts agreed upon by your respective souls, cosmic contracts sealed and signed upon the dotted line, and exciting agendas crafted with meticulous toil and care.

It's a plan filled with lessons and miracles, plot twists and turns, including those that have signed on to aggravate you and drive you silly, as how else are you to learn?

Even in instances where it's not readily apparent, there is something of value being exchanged. Perhaps, a fleeting smile that transforms your day, a compliment, or disparaging remark, scowl or the other, revealing to you – that which you do not prefer.

Each encounter is divinely simulated to flow into your life at the perfect juncture and time. Be it for a reason, a cycle or season. Even if it's a barely noticeable player loitering in the backdrop, or just some oddball stranger passing by.

Many of them are souls that you're likely connected to in a parallel life, here to support and aid your evolution in some respect. A mother, father, sibling or friend, or partner sworn to be at your side 'til perpetuity, and all the other evocative words we as humans tell ourselves.

Each relationship presents its own set of botherations, yet each is an adventure... in its own right. Each filled with ups and downs, highs and lows, and the many imposed conditions that have us bending every which way to keep the other satisfied.

*As with a ship that navigates the sea, in many ways – relationships are like unchartered territory.*
*Often we hop on board the ship with a destination in mind, I daresay.*
*Never quite knowing how long the ride will take, whether it be bumpy or steady.*
*Nevertheless, we sign up for the adventure anyway...*

Seemingly perfect strangers at the inception, presenting the most winning mask for the other to see. With the honeymoon phase ending as quickly as it started, once the facade and pretensions are dropped and more of who you both are, is revealed.

Yet, this is the very juncture when the relation starts, where the delusions fizzle and end. As, they allow the ship to move full throttle ahead. Though it may in a few cases balk and falter, or rashly come to a head.

Neither party may get what they felt they signed up for, feeling disgruntled and malcontent. Also confused. As where did the person that was to satisfy their every unfulfilled desire disappear to – the agreeable version they believed to have met?

Did you notice how different they are now compared to how they were when we first met? This is asked scoffingly, with eyes brimming with accusation and a voice tinged with rage. Though being the adept shifters that you both are, the fact that even now you're zipping through multiple realities at lightning speed, did you really expect their personas to remain unwavering? For them to be unchanged?

In this way, relationships are the perfect adventures, allowing both parties to share and explore the varying versions of themselves. More so, grow and evolve together, if this is what is truly desired. All the while holding space for the other to change and express their authentic self.

The imbalance happens when there is an insistence around how the other is supposed to act or be. With rules and rigid beliefs surrounding even how they should express their love, when our natural inclination is to be free.

For true love is not rigged with conditions, nor is it about keeping score. Nor is it about creating a running list of all the ways they've wronged you, and aspects of them you deplore. Do you recall how besotted you were in the beginning, the coquettish glances and doting stares? When it mattered less how they felt about you, as you were too wrapped up in the moment to care?

What mattered the most in that instant was the simple act of you being in the flow state. You had someone to flow your love to, though it could well have been a bird or tree. Anything that places you into the heart to where you're most aligned with who you are – which is love, as this state of grace is essentially what love is.

Are you acting from a place of grace when you scold or berate another? Or worse yet, implore and chase after them to secure their affection and care? If you are love, you can rest easily in the knowing of what you are. Moreover, you can allow that which is meant to be a part of your experience to flow towards you and resist the urge to cling to another out of desperation or fear.

What's meant for you will find you, and what's not for you...will naturally fall away. And if someone is hankering to move on from you, there's often something more sublime lurking around the corner. Though you may not believe it at the time, there's another lined up to take their place, and only too eager to stay.

Multiple soulmates for you to rendezvous with, and a multitude of experiences to be had. An entire Universe conspiring to surprise and delight you, if you'd only follow the cues, drop the resistance, and see each experience as a cosmic adventure. Or on occasion – a divine intervention, especially the ones that make you sad.

Yet even the sad ones have something to impart. Often being a stepping-stone to an interaction that is more harmonious and fulfilling. Though not by virtue of the other person being different...but more so, because you have changed.

As the ending of a thing is usually the beginning of something new. Perhaps a different outlook or shift of perspective, that radically transforms your point of view. Understand that the relationship fractured for a reason, a reason that's less about the other and more about you. For until you grasp this, and truly see the lesson that is being illuminated, the same pattern will continue to resurface until you do.

Yet, the real test of your seamanship is not how quickly you navigate the turbulent waters and take the ship to shore. But the level of ease, calm, grace, and understanding with which you're able to meet these turbulent situations – taking on board the lessons and maneuvering your ship in the direction of the flow.

Never going against the current or struggling against the tide. For sometimes the lesson is simply 'to let go'. Though the ego may well kick up a storm, as it hates when it's rejected and denied. Like a spoiled kid that acts out when it doesn't get its way, it regales you with stories. Just for the chance to prove its worth, all the while urging you to stay.

Will you heed its stories, and allow the ego to tow you around like an anchorless boat without a rudder? It does this... pulling from its clever bag of tricks to preserve its iron-clad grip of your life? Or will you acknowledge its many gambits, and choose instead to heed the glaringly obvious signals you've been ignoring all the while?

As if you're not aligned with another, why ever would you stay? Do you know, the most loving thing you can do in such instances – is the simple act of walking away?

# 13

# Art of Non-Attachment

Walk away!?

Yes, walk away! Don't loiter or waffle about, caught in a foolish quandary of your own making and second-guessing yourself at each step. Or slink away dejected, and scream and shout when nothing else works, throwing a tantrum or even worse; a pity party – just to elicit their remorse.

Moreover, do not be caught in an endless loop of questioning where you may have gone wrong. For things couldn't be any more apt. Instead, feel your emotions to the fullest, shedding a tear if it soothes your heart to do so. It's perfectly fine to grieve and be angry and feel everything there is to feel. Unless of course, you imagine a better way of releasing those lingering attachments and sentiments holding you back?

Relieve these needless hankerings and set yourself free, as the inner peace that permeates the ensuing moments can feel quite cathartic. When heated tales lose their grip, allowing you to look with ease upon these silly, soppy affairs dispassionately.

Notwithstanding, the shame and guilt that surfaces, once the dust settles, and you recall the many ways you've neglected yourself. This may give rise to mounting anger. Though you're not necessarily angry at them but yourself, for overlooking your own needs in the name of a fickled love, riddled in insecurities and abounding conditions. Deep down, you knew it was never destined to end well.

You swear like a banshee, never to engage in such frivolous tomfoolery again. But don't you worry, you'll have countless chances to put your words to the test. The experience will undoubtedly show up again. Tough not necessarily to test you, but to allow an opportunity for you to embody the lesson gained. How else is the Universe to ascertain that you've truly changed?

Yet part of the lesson is not invalidating the experience had as bad or lacking, but rather that which you've ably attracted somehow. For there are no meaningless relations. Everything happens for a reason, even if the lesson isn't very clear right now.

In the same vein – no one is inherently bad and abominable, even in the instances where they're outwardly unkind. Their seemingly brash and boorish behavior is simply how they are being, stemming from the fact that they're not aligned.

Even so, it takes two to tango, so the mere fact that you're noticing their misalignment means that you yourself may be somewhat askew. As, when you're operating from a place of balance, it's less likely for another to rankle and unsettle you.

So do not be easily jolted into action, feeling the need to match their unconscious conduct, or compromise your values to meet them where they're at. As again, we live in a vibrational universe. Any attempt to set things right via your actions rather than your frequency is a topsy-turvy stratagem, much like putting the horse before the cart.

Instead, become so aligned to where you can stand amidst a crisis, with your entire Universe appearing to crumble and crash around you. Yet you remain steadfast, not becoming unhinged by circumstances, steadily maintaining your center and cool.

You can't romp about with those that aren't vibrationally at your level, regardless of the lingering sentiment felt, or quibbling voice in your head persuading you it isn't so. Instead, you can honor and accept where they're at without trying to change them, which is key to being in flow.

To argue that it isn't so, is to haggle with Creation about how things should be. Often, it's your own ego that's doing the haggling, from its narrow perspective of what occurred or is occurring in the present moment, and stubborn insistence of how things should turn out to be.

Still, as you saunter on, know that the Universe is puffing up with pride and your guides are likely enthused – roused by your courage, and inclination to follow their cues.

Plus, letting go becomes incredibly easy, when you understand there's a larger orchestration at hand; that there's something rather delicious poised to unfold behind-the-scenes. Contrived by your inner being who sees the bigger picture and plan.

Herein, non-attachment does not mean shutting down or bottling-up your emotions, or morphing into a stone-cold, wax figure, so as not to be swayed by the external world. You know well the kind – that wouldn't dare to smile back at you in public, less their perfectly coiffured demeanor cracks and splinters, or something occurs that muddles their boundaries? Something not within their control.

For heaven forbid, they were to submit to the present moment, and just allow that which's occurring to naturally unfurl. With little to no expectations or insistence on any particular outcome – which is essentially what non-attachment is, including how others respond, or events unfold.

Not feeling the need to push, struggle, chase or implore another to bring about any particular result. You're more in a state of allowing, which is what the practice of non-resistant living is all about.

Becoming light and pliable, much like a supple grain of sand that...

*Clings to the rock for a bit... then bit by bit falls away.*

*Not tied or tethered to anything, and gracefully surrendering to the sweeping surge of the torrent underway.*

*Becoming one with the water, and the briny, fathomless depths of the sea.*

*Trusting deeply in the intelligence of the cosmos, feeling curious, feeling light, and moreover feeling blissfully free.*

You embrace all that unfolds with the naïve optimism and near-bullish faith of a two-year old, which is the level of unquestioning conviction to have. With the utmost trust that what you're experiencing is for your highest good. As your inner being would never intentionally steer you towards an experience that veers you off the intended path.

It's always guiding you, especially in the instances that feel challenged and strained. Like when you're reeling from a break-up that's left you crushed and bitter, and agonizing over your wounds. Not to mention the countless injustices sustained.

Everyone has a story; some harrowing ordeal that they've had to pull through that propelled their expansion, and as such – was not borne in vain. Even so, do you imagine the Universe to deliver to you, what's been promptly queued up for you and waiting, when the vibration you're offering is punctuated by hurt and pain?

## 14

# Releasing Hurt & Pain

*But I'm not hurting. I'm doing fine! I really am!*

This is a story that you've repeated time and time again, to where it becomes a knee-jerk declaration of invincibility. It's a story that's spewed to anyone enquiring about your well-being, those close enough to have an inkling of the recent anguish faced.

Each word is uttered with more deliberation to where they evoke admiration... leaving no doubt to the imagination of those present – that you've indeed moved on.

Yet even as you voice this tale, inwardly – you know well the sting of the unrelenting pain. How your heart aches and flutters when your mind traitorously wanders in spite attempts to restrain it, step by creaking step, down memory lane.

There's the internal scuffle that follows, to tamp down the unwanted thoughts that leap and caper unchecked on the walls of your mind, before retreating once again like ghoulish specters. They elicit feelings of nostalgia that leave you feeling agitated and somewhat unhinged, betraying the lingering sentiments and trepidation within.

Not even the insistent pitch of your voice is loud enough to drown out the protesting shrieks of your conscience – when your inner world is replete with so many rousing thoughts that never seem to wane.

Long after you've gathered the pictures and mementos and lit a fire to them, that crackled like a raging inferno, the flames of which held the promise of setting ablaze and emancipating your pain. Even so, the effusive memories remain.

Though, if you're being honest, a small part of you secretly treasures them. These tear-jerking memorabilia; clinging to this fragile repository of cloying stories. If not, why would you nourish them with your attention – continue to water them with your tears?

Your own secret time capsule that you alone have access to and can revisit time and time again. Without the world being aware of these mental transgressions, and the countless schemes and unfulfilled scenarios running rampant in your brain.

Yet how can you escape this emotional ordeal, if you continue to relive and recreate the past? For the mind, as shrewd and clever as it may be – cannot discern the present from the past. As such, it chalks up these evocative musings, as experiences that are unfolding this very instant.

Still, the only reason you may have held on to these stories is that you perceive them to benefit you in some way. Perhaps deep down, there's a belief that you may not fare better or find someone equally or more attractive. With this limiting doubt holding your much-anticipated manifestations at bay.

Even if they are as captivating as you make them out to be, are you not a rarity too? A one-of-a-kind diamond, that sparkles and shines especially when under pressure. Why? Do you imagine that there's another in existence quite like you?

As again, how can another see you, when simply put – you're remiss at seeing yourself? Too busy putting them on a pedestal, when the very qualities you see in them that evoke your admiration, mean you must contain these qualities as well.

Given that they're such a reflective mirror, means that the reverse is also true. For oft times, those that lash out and inflict hurt upon another are themselves hurting. Though their trauma and lack of alignment has entirely nothing to do with you.

Perhaps they were bullied as a child, and now as an adult, have an unfavorable reaction to those they perceive as timid or weak. With the very sight of one that appears disempowered reminding them of their own vulnerability; an aspect of themselves they quite despise... that part of them that's not fully healed.

Or they may themselves have experienced rejection, deemed clingy and possessive by someone they adored. With the encounter serving as a huge afront to their ego, to where your own neediness reminds them of their past desperation. As such, causing them to push you away, out of annoyance and fear.

In this way, those that mistreat and inflict hurt on others often lack compassion for themselves. How then do you expect them to give you, what they do not have to give?

If hearing this does nothing to appease your ego, and you're still seeking revenge or an apology for things left unsaid and undone. Understand that no amount of haggling over past injustices can undo the momentum of what's already been done.

Even so, I know well how you feel; the searing anger, the humiliation, and overwhelming sense of hopelessness when things don't quite go as planned. All valid emotions. Though the real affront is not what they've done to you, but rather what you've done to yourself. It's you, using their misbehavior to justify your own lack of alignment, by what you've chosen to fixate on.

With the very attention, amplifying within you, the vibration of that which you seek to overcome. The truth is – you'll never be satisfied, if your remedy for feeling better lies within the control of another, perhaps a half-baked apology or some other loquacious display of remorse. For true contentment arises only when those external to you, no longer have the power to rattle or unsettle your inner world.

Knowing this, you can look upon them with compassion, without feeling wronged or incensed. Which is not to say becoming a doormat for their mistreatment. as you can lovingly sidestep their antics, and if it soothes you to do so – elect to walk away instead.

While you may empathize with what they're experiencing, their pain and angst aren't your crosses to bear. Moreover, walking away may well be the best thing you can do for them. For it reveals that there are consequences for their misbehavior, should they have the wherewithal to care.

Even so, another person cannot hurt you or cause you anguish unless you give your power away. So, what belief do you hold of them to set them on such a peerless pedestal, or perhaps of yourself – to undermine yourself in that way?

Furthermore, all pain is an indication of the innate resistance that you feel, be a false belief you're holding on to, or lesson that you stubbornly refuse to heed.

With every fiber of your being clamoring for your attention; that ache in your feet when you're barking up the wrong path, or unsettling feeling in your gut that wouldn't recede. Finally, reaching an ear-splitting pitch, before ceding with a grunt of resignation eventually giving way to some form of lamentable affliction or disease.

And now that it's got your attention, you're all eyes and ears....

Your brain short-circuits to a single stream of thinking, fixating on the very thing that your body has been prompting you all the while to avoid. So focused on the discomfort – that you miss the learning. Caught in a seemingly endless loop of self-sabotage and overthinking, as what you focus on unknowingly expands and thrives.

Even so, I know how defiant the mind can be when in the throes of an affliction, to where your body is constantly railing, and rebelling at every turn. It's quite a harrowing task to dismantle the bedrock of dysfunctional beliefs – the root of all your anguish. Yet the minute they're debunked, the issue will fade away and be gone.

Though debunked, not with the intent to invalidate – but simply expose them as the untrue notions that they are. The mere fact that you're having the experience means it's there to serve a purpose, even if it unfolds in a manner, you do not prefer.

Each tribulation, however difficult, is occurring to expand you in some way. As what would be the point of a pristine, spotless experience anyway? Do you imagine your inner being to be that unimaginative and dull?

If your ears are agape with interest and sufficiently ajar – hear this and hear this well. The cure to many a woe, is not to tussle with your stubborn thoughts, or submit to the grim fate of being unwell. But as best as you are able, intentionally reach for the feel-good moments. Bit by bit your willful mind will acquiesce.

For the heart is the motherboard, and when activated, the mind will simmer down. By doing more of the things that transport you into the heart space. As, when your inner oasis is in harmonic balance, your outer reality will undoubtedly transform.

Before you know it, you'll feel light and unfettered again. You'll look back with utter credulity, and wonder – whatever took you so long?

# <u>15</u>

# *Birthing Yourself Anew*

Indeed! What for heaven's sake took you so long?

Took you so very long to bridge the gap between you and the more expanded you. The version of you that you've secretly mused and fantasized about, as you too must have a vision. Something you're desiring to birth into existence. The very thought of which adds a pep to your step... that incites and spurs you on.

And don't for a second, imagine yourself to be the exception, or give me the trite, pathetic spiel about being well past your prime. Or lament, that you're well beyond the age where things excite and thrill you. Lulled into inaction by a world that will at every turn, try to convince you of the dangers of indulging your inner child.

When excitement, as you now know, happens to be the language of your soul.

With your higher mind, in every moment, showering you with a ready stream of ideas for you to act upon. Yet if you steadily ignore this communion to where you're expressing not as a complete but fragmented being, how then do you expect to feel coherent and whole?

This is not to imply that you're in any way broken, inadequate or tethering on the verge of mortal decline. Yet, a soul that's continuously starved of creative expression will eventually stagnate, to where it feels like you're slowly wilting and withering away from the inside.

Drifting apathetically to the mundane yet familiar rhythm; all the while being the perfect puppet to someone else's drum. As, do you recall who it was that sold you on the incredibly foolish scheme of ceding your freedom to appease the whims of another? Or filled your ears with empty promises of a utopian future and other sweet nothings, enticing enough to tempt many-an-unsuspecting man.

You peg away to the point of exhaustion, feeling underwhelmed – or worse yet spent and fatigued. Too jaded to care, or even notice what you're becoming or the unrecognizable specter of your former self you've unheedingly become.

Empty days that seem to drag on, marked by a subliminal clock, but it's not like anyone is keeping score – or vigil. Of the countless hours spent in robotic deference, punctuated by quick dopamine fixes. Until sleep mercifully covets your consciousness, only to awaken to the same humdrum, run-of-the-mill routine yet again.

With the unchanging dance becoming more tedious and uncomfortable with time. It comes to a screeching halt only when the aching void of your own abandonment reaches a screaming crescendo, that lands you amid what feels like an existential crisis. You then question your purpose, and all the many ways in which you've bungled your life.

The initial turmoil gives way to a sort of hollow acceptance of things past and yet to come, having grown complacent and cautious. It's an enduring wariness that has etched itself deep into your consciousness. It's rendered you somewhat skeptical of anything too fanciful, like the pie-in-the-sky prospect of turning your life around.

Even so, wherever you find yourself – be it disgruntled employee, disillusioned retiree or impressionable naïve. It's never too late to dispel the self-doubt holding you back from being your fullest expression, as then and only then will the entirety of what is lined up for you spontaneously fall into place.

For it's not that the Universe abandoned you, as it's always on your side. It holds its breath in agog anticipation of the moment that you'll harken to the promptings of your inner being. When you answer the call to step fully into your purpose, regardless of age, past hangups, or the sordid deck of cards you feel you've been dealt so far in life.

Deep down, the tiny voice of your ego may pipe up, quivering from the impending shift that threatens to disrupt the familiar rhythm of its unwavering world. The ego hates change. But what's the worst that can happen? Do you fear that a bit of adventure will flip your neat, cookie-cutter existence, upside down?

Even so, a tiny spark of rebellion flickers, igniting the flame of passion within you, that's been lying dormant all the while. It sets the stage for a more exciting chapter to unfold. For you to tell a more empowered story by virtue of what you are being, as knowledge devoid of action creates stagnation – rendering your abilities utterly futile.

As is a singer that's lost their chops still a vocalist, or an artist that sits on their gifts; allowing them to mold and fester, worthy of creating art? Furthermore, can you qualify as anything, if what you profess to be and what you're being... are worlds apart?

Natheless, the question isn't whether you're creating, but rather, what you're birthing into this world. And whether you're doing so by acting out someone else's ideals or ideas, or your own – by tuning in to the promptings of your heart?

Nothing that animates and excites you should ever be averted or postponed. Not habitually anyway. For if you continue to disregard these willful cues sent by your inner being and cosmic team, what incentive do they have to send you more?

And if not now – when? Are you waiting until you feel ready enough, seen enough and know all the right steps, parts and pieces, and is motivated enough... to even begin?

Yet if you find yourself plain dithering and devoid of ideas with nowhere to start. How about pivoting the mirror around a bit? Start by relinquishing the limiting beliefs keeping you stuck, and really taking the time to do the self-work.

Often, it's not a lack of foresight or wit that's holding you back. But a crippling sense of self-preservation that causes you to shrink away into the tiny, unassuming box you've carved out for yourself. So very adept at dimming your light, for fear of being judged.

Even so, every noteworthy creation ever made began with a vision, and even the most illustrious of artists or avant-garde scientists have a muse. Something that aspires or kindles your imagination, even if that muse happens to be you.

As the most versatile palette that you'll ever work with is the one immediately within your control. So, if you're still racking your brain for a jump off point, you'll find the following practice to be a most helpful and a rather effective stepping-stone.

...........................................

*Find a quiet corner to sit in, where no one may disturb your peace.*

*Grab a pen and paper and start by making a list, albeit not a terribly long one –*

*Of all the things about yourself, and changes you'd like to see.*

*Perhaps healthy hair, clearer skin, or feeling more... nimble and spry*

*Do not hold back, as this is really the time to go out on a limb.*

*By really stretching your imagination and mind.*

*Once the list is done and dusted, it's time to quiet your mind.*

*By sitting still, and visualizing every minute detail of the new you,*

*you're looking to birth to life.*

*Dropping the image when sufficiently excited, and allowing the Universe*
*to further embellish your design. It undoubtedly will – if you just give it time.*

Time and faith, as nothing ever takes shape in physical reality, where there's a vacuum of trust. Trust that the Universe is always earnestly working in your favor. Moreover, trust in your own mastery, as even now you're birthing multiple realities with your imagination, so why not take a gamble on you? Isn't it worth the fuss?

Keep in mind that the transformed version of you cannot be sired in the past. So, if you're forever mulling over the many unpleasing scenarios that led to this moment, detail after feverish detail. Or chastising yourself for the countless humiliations endured and how in hindsight you would've preferred to act. You're doing yourself a tremendous disservice, though you may well be oblivious to this fact.

The thing is, the mind cannot tell the difference between past and present, and believes the experience is happening now. So, each time you revisit those unsettling memories, you unknowingly recreate within you – a vibration that keeps you stuck.

Yet with every rebirth, there's some preparation to be had, that aids you to relinquish those pesky habits and tendencies. Not to mention, the crippling pangs of self-condemnation spawned from aged memories that hold you prisoner to yesterday's past.

So, if ready to let go of the old patterns holding you back? There're a few titillating tips about guilt and shame in the lines that follow... that will empower you to do just that.

# *16*

# *Releasing Guilt & Shame*

How many times have you flipped over backwards, jumping through endless hoops – the ultimate trapezist, riddled by the shame and guilt of saying no?

Your mind churning every which way, coming up with a million ruses to maneuver your way out of the jamb you've somehow managed to hedge yourself into. All the artfully crafted excuses flying out the window the next instant, as you watch in rapt disbelief, as your own mouth, almost as if of its own volition – give you away.

You find yourself mouthing words that are not altogether unfamiliar, reaffirmed by a nod of approval, inward sigh of resignation... and that strained, unconvincing smile. All this, as you give in to the unshakeable urge to appear selfless... the overwhelming impulse to be liked.

Yet, no matter how many times you act out this saint-like charade, it does nothing to quell the disquiet felt inside. The knowing deep within – that you've deceived yourself in some unspeakable way. For sin is not some vile, ignoble act done to undermine or harm another, but rather the act of abandoning yourself.

It's a feeling that stays with you. Long after the short-lived satisfaction of appearing a martyr fades, and you're left to carry out the action that you've grudgingly signed up for. Promises that now weighs heavily upon you like a mantle on your shoulder, evoking feelings of bitterness, rancor and rage.

Though fret not – as every act is an act of self-love, even in the instances that you're seemingly abandoning your own needs... which may sound a tad cliché.

Seen another way, isn't altering your words and behavior to win the favor of another not the classic manipulative tactic, even if not executed in the most wholesome of ways? Or minding your words, and tiptoeing on eggshells so as not to rattle and upset another just so they feel safe to linger at your side, not another ploy to get them to stay?

It stems from countless years of conditioning, believing your self-worth to be tied to how others respond. Else, why is it so important for them to like you, or even stick around? Would your world, as you know it, really unravel and fall apart if others were to perceive you as cold and selfish? Or whatever apt labels they may call you, when you're not giving in to peer-pressure, stroking their egos, or overly concerned with fitting in.

Not to mention, its sheer insanity to try to make another happy at the expense of your own bliss. Yet do elevate others, if it genuinely pleases your heart to do so — as the misalignment only occurs when you're doing so grudgingly, feeling put out and remiss. Though, by no means do so against your will. As remaining clammed-up and silent to avoid an external conflict will only serve to incite a war within yourself.

A flurry of guilt, which simply put, is a coping mechanism. A carryover from the petulant inner child that did not perhaps feel loved and seen, and as such, might have had to pander and fawn to receive its parent's love and assent.

At the heart of which is the false belief that you're somehow responsible for how others around you feel. Or that you need to appear nice and agreeable to avoid judgment or worse yet punishment. Consequentially not giving yourself permission to express, in a manner that's authentic and real.

When truth be told, you can never be sweet enough to soothe another or loving enough to secure their love. Perhaps you've had the experience where you've strove hard to get another to see and appreciate your worth. Only for them to forsake you upon the appearance of someone deemed more favorable, dismissing you at the drop of a hat.

Even so, the guilt and shame felt are certainly valid, though not for the reason conceived. Serving instead to illuminate the whimsical ideals of perfection you've been holding on to – all hankerings of a persona, fixated on controlling how it's perceived.

With the slightest departure from these ideals seen as offending and tactless. Not to mention the self-orchestrated gaslighting. Truth be told, no one's pointing fingers, and we're often our own worse judge and critic. In fact, what if the guilt and shame felt has nothing to do with acts of misdeeds against others, but misalignment with yourself?

That deep inner shame that arises when, in your illusory quest for perfection, you've meandered off the intended path. As, the quest to be perfect is a rather futile one; one that hinders your expansion. Which is not to say there're no insightful takeaways or lessons to be had. However, true expansion arises by honoring exactly who and where you are.

It's recognizing that you're already perfect as you are, though this truth is little understood. As, does the man that's financially abundant yearn for monetary riches, or someone healthy feel void of health? By the same token, do you truly possess... that which you quest for? The mere fact that you are hankering after it – tells me you do not.

Though not in the literal sense of the word, as you are perfect whether you believe it or not. Even so, to entertain the thought that you are, may seem a great affront to the ego – and underlying belief system, that habitually tries to shut down your self-worth.

Yet, the minute you acknowledge this to be true, these illusory beliefs will give way, and the niggling self-judgment will disperse. It will provide fresh clarity and fill you with newfound resolve, and perspective that you did not previously have.

You'll come to realize that you are indeed worthy, even in the instances where your actions may be less than pristine. The very fact that they gave you pause hints at an underlying nature that is inherently well-intended and kind. So, there's never a need to beat up and chastise yourself. For if you never messed up, how then are the earthly lessons that allow you to continually refine your preferences, ever to be gleaned?

And while the prospect of saying no, standing your ground and putting your own needs ahead of others may feel a bit daunting, you'd never rid yourself of these needless emotions without the necessary practice. A new way of being wouldn't suddenly magic itself into existence via wishful thinking, or simply through sheer force of will.

Moreover, no amount of complying can please another or get them to see your perspective – let alone understand you, if you're not operating on the same wavelength. Though you sure can try. Saddled with the need to explain and justify your actions in earnest and apologize at the mere whiff of a looming conflict. Just so, you may absolve yourself of their reproof, less they find you lacking or bereft.

Yet a word of precaution, is the provisional pat on the back and brownie points, truly worth the effort – and price of sacrificing your integrity, peace and health?

# 17

# To Heal, To Render Whole

Healing in *Hebrew* means to make whole... to restore to normality, and the latter couldn't be any less apt. In that, no amount of pandering to the whims of a conditioned society can render you normal, if what you're being is all an act.

Granted it being a rather seemly performance. For as soon as you're able to talk, you're given a rulebook with strict rules on how you're to walk, talk and act, with the lofty expectation of you towing the line. As heaven forbid, you were to stray from this carefully polished set of acceptable norms or dare to color outside the line.

*But you wouldn't do that, would you? You're such a well-behaved obedient child.*

Your forebearers were clearly visionary and far-seeing thinkers, ensuring to plan and strategize for every deviant scenario down the line. For a single wayward act, thought or misstep – and you'd find yourself sitting squarely before a shrink or the other, as it takes just one bad apple to tarnish the entire batch, given time.

Someone well versed and able to dissect and decipher every offending aspect of your personality... each abnormal curvature or iffy tendency of your mind. One capable of crafting the perfect diagnosis; the most fitting sedative to dumb you down and nip your wayward behavior in the bud. Before you know it you'll be restored to normality, pliant and popping like all the other apples about you. No one looking would have an inkling there was ever a blemish, or even chance to tell you alike.

Though why be normal aka ordinary, when you can be extraordinary; decidedly different and unapologetically outlandish, at the risk of being criticized or rebuked? Never seeking to blend in nor pausing to see what anyone else thinks. Regardless of whether they find you quaint or kooky, giving little credence to their opinions of you.

This would probably be pretty good advice, except that you likely wouldn't heed it anyway. Like most, you probably need to go through the school of hard knocks and emerge bruised and battered to arrive at the very conjecture, I dare say.

Which is the point of life. As words do not teach, only experience does. Much like a toddler that learns to walk by repeatedly falling, only to pick itself back up again. With no ornate handbook other than its own innate guidance system to guide it. For isn't this what true mastery is?

Does the wind ever pause to wonder which way to blow, or a tree – ponder on which way to sway? Plus, we need only to gaze upon nature; the creeping vines that amble about in riotous abandon and bats that hibernate on without end, never caring to fit in or tamp down their natural instincts, to get a whiff of what normalcy is.

Yet, we're so quick to cede our sovereignty to others, believing they know what's best for us. When truthfully, they haven't got a clue. So many, eager to dole out a solution and rattle off a list of tried and proven dos and don'ts that's worked for them, assuming it will also work for you. Though, they've never stood a day in your shoes.

As such, they're utterly oblivious of what is right and acceptable for you.

Shouldn't normalcy be defined then, not by the prudish rules imposed by society, but whether the experience sought aligns with your highest purpose? A purpose, if you agree – is known only to your higher self, and to a degree subconsciously by you.

Even so, you'll know when something is right by the quality of ease felt, or via a lack of it, which you'll undoubtedly learn. As it's only by trying on and trudging around the weighty expectations and thrifted ideologies of those around you, that were never yours anyway, would you have reason to set them down.

Finally getting to the point where you leave all others out of the equation, and craft your own definition of normalcy based on what feels seamless and natural to you. For true healing begins at the juncture where self-judgment ends. When you're wholly ready to dismantle the false notions of wholeness pilfered from others, realizing you're already perfect. In fact, there was never anything to fix or refashion within you.

With this realization, all diseases, stemming from a lack of ease, will fall away, requiring no elaborate remedies, magic bullets or pills. All that's really needed is to restore the balance of your system by eliminating the root of the agitation and fear.

Still, it is your prized avatar, which means you get to primp and pamper it at will. With no act of self-care being excessive or trifling, as when the cells of your body are at ease and soothed you can't help but feel hale, and healthful as well. Though the reverse is also true. For when strung out or stressed, the tension felt will echo throughout your being – unsettling your cells, that can't help but share in your malaise too.

Natheless, there are a few must-haves that are required to bring the body into a natural state of homeostasis, and for its optimal upkeep. Just as a plant requires light, water and oxygen to sustain it, you need these too. This entails movement, to keep the energetic field of your body flowing, not omitting... good quality food, rest and sleep.

So, the question isn't whether you're nourishing the body, but more a matter of whether you're doing it well. Though not via mindless adherence to the conditioned programs – same that lead you to believe you need eight hours of sleep or cups of water. But by heeding your bodily impulses; the palpable aches and pains, and insistent rumbles of discomfort that you persistently tamp down and go out on a limb to quell.

In fact, if you were to become devilishly still and tune in, your body will let you know the instant it's dehydrated or fatigued... and could really use some rest.

Or when starved for good-quality nutrition, though not on occasion of being famished or underfed. Still, can you in good conscience say that your body is adequately nourished if you're habitually feeding it with processed food loaded with toxins? It's no secret that such poisons pollute your cells, rendering them unable to absorb the nutrients from foods you ingest.

Yet, we are by and large a product of our environment, which if we care to admit, isn't as pristine and pure as it could be. Given how polluted things are, detoxing your body regularly to remove the build-up of toxins from your cells with special herbs that may support this, is key.

It requires a small change of habit, paying notice to not just what you consume, but also how you breathe. You're clearly alive – so you're unarguably taking in air. But do you know that most humans are habitual shallow breathers, neglecting that deep belly breathing that's so essential to revive the cells and enable cellular repair?

Even so, no amount of ingested sustenance would be as effective without a daily dibble of sunlight. It's no wonder you feel morose and uptight. As the body was contrived to play and frolic freely in nature. Unless you deem it natural to be housed up from dawn to dust amidst the concrete walls within which you work and reside? Barely

setting foot outside, and habitually submerged in a heady stream of artificial lights.

Not to mention the lack of movement, sitting sedentary, hour upon fleeting hour, rendered motionless in the contraptions you call chairs. Yet, exercise is crucial to sustain the flow of your vital lifeforce energy, which may grow stagnant from inertia, resulting in energetic blockages that may show up in the body as some manner of malaise.

Just as well, if upon hearing this, your body is physically impaired or constrained. There's a powerful visualization technique shared later that's most effective at loosening any blocks, no matter the state of your body, to get your energy moving freely again.

No matter the level of dilly-dallying, flagrant neglect – or indifference, there's no sidestepping the essential act of self-care. For taking responsibility for you entails taking account for the whole of you, by making time for your health and welfare.

So, if you're not already doing so, why? Aren't you deserving of being prioritized? Or have you lost sight of what's important, feeling that the monetary rewards gained by stressing and straining – heedless of your wellbeing, are truly worth the price?

When wholeness is valuing and seeing worth in every facet of your being, from the texture of your hair, lilt of your voice, to the not-so-pleasing aspects of your persona, that are oft times frowned upon. As, if there're any aspects of you that's left out of the equation, is your notion of yourself... indeed a holistic one?

Loving all the parts of you deemed unlovable that perhaps were past reviled and spurned. For as much as healing cannot ensue from a place of lack and inadequacy, infirmity cannot endure in a space of wholeness and unflagging self-worth.

Knowing this, isn't the precursor to wholeness the result of realizing your worth?

# <u>18</u>

# *Valuation of the Self*

Moreover, realizing how cherished you are....

Utterly beloved, by an inner being that adores you. Not to mention your cosmic team. If you had the slightest whiff or inkling of just how magical you appeared to them; a beautiful, luminous light – resplendent and dazzling in all your glory, you'd never utter an unkind word or judge yourself harshly again.

Self-deprecating lies, masquerading under the guise of you being impartial and accepting. Yet accepting by whose standards exactly? A largely clueless society – schooled to embrace crippling notions of beauty, that accredits value based on how one looks and acts. Or personal wealth, and other such material trappings amassed.

With everyone vying for the same things, chasing after fanciful ideas of abundance, and wanting to be more. More affluent, thinner, prettier or better esteemed. At the heart of which is an intense need to be appreciated – and more importantly, to be seen.

A bottomless well of repressed emotions, tamped down for fear of appearing clingy. In so doing, creating a whirlpool of inner conflict that rails and rages within.

Momentarily appeased by short lived bouts of acclaim. Fleeting words of praise in the wake of hurtling around to prove how hardworking you are. Or perhaps, that steady stream of impassioned adulation, feverishly uttered in the throes of a one-night stand.

No vice, too extreme or too much...

Yet once the moment fades, with a resounding thud, you're right back where you started – resuming the familiar dance that mirrors the aching void felt, when alone. No measure of attention, however soothing in an instance, can gratify you. For it's not their acknowledgment that you truly need, but your own.

It stems from an utter failure to see yourself. The searing self-loathing and neglect felt, mercilessly wrangling away the things that give you joy, with your sense of morale and self-worth ripped to shreds.

Tattered and torn, and in a state of disrepair. Even so, no one can put back together and mend your worth, as only you alone can do this. With lavish flattery and praises serving only as a band-aid. Just like a flimsy tape straining to hold together the pieces of a shattered ego. Your inner child, pliant and dejected from years of abasement, having grown accustomed to being overlooked, the lack of self-apathy and disdain.

*As, each time you mask and disguise yourself, you are saying to your inner child that it is not worthy of being seen.*

*Each time you mute yourself when you feel the urge to speak up, you are saying to your inner child that it's not deserving... of being heard.*

*Finally, each time you chastise and judge yourself, you are demeaning your inner child ... which does little in the way of affirming your worth.*

In short, we're often the villain and victim of our stories – oft times being our own worst critic. So very adept at putting yourself last. How then can you expect to win?

Win at the game of being your true self, which in its purest form, is unconditional love and light. And not seek it in another. As only those that are well rooted in being and hold themselves in the utmost regard, can truly see another. A rarity these days. With many vying to be seen and appreciated, when the world is replete with deeply wounded and insecure people. Not to mention, you cannot receive from another, that which you do not to a degree, yourself contain.

Plus, if everyone is seeking high and low for the same thing, who will be the one to embody it and bring this much sought-after, elusive love into the world?

Moreover, you never want to go seeking warmth in those dark, somber and secluded places. But rather, remain steadfast where you are. This allows those that have been long shrouded in their amnesic blankets to catch a glimpse of your light burning ever so brightly before them. Before you know it, they'll be tempted to step towards you. For a lighthouse can be an eyesore to ships trapped within the murky waters of a turbulent sea... or have lost their way in the wake of a storm.

Not very long ago, I had a dream...

I was walking up a stairwell lined with people, the likes of which you cannot imagine. They were malnourished and starving, malformed and twisted. I felt empathy, but at the same time, an overwhelming urge to escape.

Yet as I hurried on by, an inner voice within my head, said *look...look at them.*

I turned to look upon the one closest to me. She was very young – a mere child. As I looked at her, I saw that she was shining and glowing quite luminously. Her eyes, much like radiant, reflective pools in her tiny face. Clear, bright saucers brimming with a purity and innocence that I had not noticed before. They reflected not just her pure and angelic nature, but I realized then that she wanted or needed nothing, except to be seen.

There was a spark of light coming from her center of her forehead – the God spark. I could see this light. As I turned to look at each of them in turn, the illusory façade of their unkempt and startling appearances fell away. Each had a similar spark that emanated from their third eye, and all together, they lit up like the most amazing Christmas tree.

The tree of life itself; with its branches extended towards the heavens, and its roots firmly anchored in the ground below. An army of God's angels, gazing upwards at me, and inviting me to look beyond their exterior forms to the pure essence and luminous nature within. All lined up and patiently waiting – all the while desiring to be seen.

My heart expanded with understanding and love. My feet slowed its hurried and impatient staccato on the steps. The veil fell away from my eyes, allowing me to gaze into the most beautiful mirrors yet. Mirrors that have been scattered about and readily available the whole time. Becoming visible to me, the instant that I was willing to set aside my well stitched-up preconceived notions and take a closer look at myself.

As again, it's never about whether others can see you, and all about whether you can see yourself. I invite you now, to see the light that you are. even when the world does not. More so, continue to tend to the flickering flame of unconditional love within you, when all other lights blink out.

See this light also in others, as their essential nature – which is light, remains intact, even in the instances when they've forgotten who they are. For it takes only one example; one clear and unsullied mirror, to reflect to them just how truly beautiful they are. When you do, they will gaze upon you and will not be able to tear their eyes away from what they are seeing, as they've never seen anything quite like it before. So go out, shine your light and be a beacon of radiance within the world.

Be the Angel that you naturally are. The perfect looking glass. Allow yourself to stare head-on at your own reflection with renewed understanding and compassion. Keep in mind, if the external world does not appear to value you, it may well be that you haven't yet fully embraced your own value. If so, can you imagine a more ideal time to start?

By this, I do not mean your future self; the version of you after you've gone to the gym and lost the uncomely weight. Or version thereafter, once you've landed the dream job and finally bagged that illustrious career. But the person that's you are right now. This is the version; I invite you to wholly embrace.

Your physical attributes are no doubt beautiful, but like everything else, your exterior form will also change. So even if you were to meet that far-fetched beauty standard in the next instant, is it a façade that you can realistically sustain?

Knowing this, do you really want to tie your worth to something so changeable? It would be akin to building your house on the sand, requiring a mere breeze to topple the entire structure, and your impermanent world along with it. So why invest in something so fickle, when you can shift your focus to the aspects of your being that sustain?

By asking yourself this question. Who are you, when all the titles and accolades are stripped away?

Which is not to discount the preciousness of your avatar. Yet, how can you know yourself if you do not conceive the whole of self, that is so much more than just your persona... your body, and pair of eyes registering these words?

# _19_

# _Know Thy Self_

That's right! You are the innate consciousness that is perceiving these words.

Call it higher self, inner being, lifeforce energy – whatever label feels most resonant and apt. It's the aspect of your consciousness that's focused, in such a way to allow for the physical reality experience. Being such a masterful focuser, it's no surprise it's taken those on your planet a good many jaunts around the moon to finally wake up.

Though awaken you indeed have, especially if you find yourself here, eager to find out more about this seemingly arcane godly being. Whom, for ages you've been regaled with tales of it being outside and apart from you. When in fact, you're one and the same.

There's no differentiating Creation – in its totality, from your soul. No set point where one starts and the other begins, but rather a matter of focus. With your soul to a larger extent focused, though not exclusively, in your direction... and Creation not.

Being multidimensional, what reason would the soul have to limit its perspective when it may experience various facets of itself simultaneously – expressed as your many parallel selves?

It would be like flipping a die with multiple faces but restricting your view to a single side. When each side reflects a unique number that holds within it a different meaning, a different outcome – in this intriguing game called life.

Parallel selves... parallel lives; the many personality instances of your soul that exist in realms and realities that are typically invisible to the naked eye. Even so, there's a common thread interlacing all these selves to allow you to telepathically share and relay information gleaned with each other. Can you imagine a more magnificent design?

Each parallel version aids the expression of a different persona and point of view. While existing in differing dimensions, each also has access to the wisdom and acumen amassed by the whole of you. Yet, each is tasked with its own unique mission or cosmic pursuit, to explore themes most pivotal to the soul, allowing this multifaceted adventure to ensue. So, that the soul is universal, is undoubtedly true.

It exists everywhere. Which is not to say the attention of your inner being is limited, or that you are in any way ignored. Being that it's not restricted by space and time, it's able to perceive all these realities simultaneously. As such, it's always at your beck and call.

Even now...

Ready to steer and council you, if you'd only heed its promptings.

It transmits wave upon wave of pulsating signals that gyrate to the entrancing rhythm of these faint yet palpable cues that reverberate through the heart. Did I not say that the heart is the motherboard? It's the gateway through which all communication from the higher self is acutely felt, if attuned enough to intercept its meaning. For the meaning may well be lost, if these cues are disregarded or little understood.

Like that lamentable ick you feel when you look upon another, that may well be spewing anger and hate. Yet it isn't so much your intuition signaling that the other is bad. But rather, the misalignment felt stemming from you being completely out of sync with that higher-self aspect of you. As your inner being sees the other only through the lens of compassion, with not the merest whiff of judgment or pronouncement of guilt.

Your emotions in this instance act as a barometer to let you know that you're somewhat off-kilter with who you innately are. So, you may regard these unpredictable bouts of energy that explode and erupt unheralded at your core, as your own secret love language between you and your higher self. It's your inner being's way of signaling when you're astray and amiss, assuming you have the wherewithal to hear.

For whom you are at the core – is undoubtedly love. But is it enough to intellectually know this, if you are reacting to the world around you with condemnation?

The instance you judge another, you become the vibration of judgment itself. Can you then, in good conscience say that you are love, if what you are being moment to moment, is something else?

Even in the instances where you're not condemning others, can you calibrate to the loving frequency that is your core vibration – if you're off in a corner being mopish and sullen, chastising and judging yourself?

Completely captivated by the very reality you've created, that you've somehow forgotten that it is a mirage. The external world exists to provide a context within which you can express and discover more of who you are. However, if distracted by petty preoccupations, this could prove a rather daunting task.

Which brings us full circle to the reason you're here... abuzz and bristling

with a hankering to know and fulfill the agenda of your soul. It's an agenda known only to you, albeit subconsciously. It entails the quest to not only discover but become more of your higher self, which may at present seem a rather lofty goal.

Yet feasible, no doubt! Granted it may require a bit of self-enquiry, though not in a fanatical sense. Eyes agog, edgily scrutinizes everything. Now that you're tasked with the cliffhanging mission of rediscovering and finally coming home to yourself.

It demands that you shift a portion of your focus and direct this attention within. In so doing, you'll be much more mindful of your inclinations to the earthy impulses – the subconscious programs; forebodings and triggers. For once illuminated by the light of your awareness, they'll lose their power to unsettle you... time and time again.

Bit by bit, you'll come to know yourself. Which is not to say that the process of knowing the self, given that your soul is in a constant state of expansion and evolution, has a definitive end. But the more attuned you are to your core self, the more of who you are will reveal itself to you. Before you know it – a doorway to your inner world will crack open, rocketing you into unspeakable bliss.

It will afford you access to extrasensory perceptions and experiences that are beyond the grasp of the physical senses. The mysteries of which remain inexhaustible, that you may get an inkling of, herein.

You see, to really fathom the multi-dimensional being that you are requires a sound grasp of the operative context you're existentially in. Though it isn't so much that you are a product of your outer environment, but your inner one.

Would it not then behoove you to acquaint yourself with the principles governing this vast and intricate universe, that unfurls and extends in every direction within?

## <u>20</u>

# *Mastering the Universal Game*

Don't tell me, the Universe has rules too!?

Words tinged with a hint of disappointment straddled the air for what felt like an agonizing second, followed by a dispirited grunt.

Yet if you're shirking away like a sullen child, listen up. These aren't just your typical rules – designed to pilfer your freedom. Another set of laws crafted with little regard for preserving your autonomy, granted that freedom is undeniably your birthright, or other such compelling edict for you to mindlessly adopt.

Which is not to say that all such precedents are bad and corrupt.

If you were to reflect to the most enticing game ever played, would it not be a drawback if you're oblivious to the rules? What odds say, would there be to win?

The fact that in this moment you are immersed in a game may come as a bit of a surprise. A universal game – with curveballs and pitfalls, smokescreens and ploys... and a convincing lineup of characters, that you are playing even now, wittingly or otherwise.

Yet the catch twist is that there are no opponents, nor coveted destination in sight. Moreover, it's your call whether or not to navigate this cosmic maze unseeingly. As

you know, there's an invincible team guiding you, and are always at your side.

Even so, having an awareness of these principles will prove a game changer, if the prospect of taking charge of your reality thrills you. Moreover, having the discernment on when to act or go with the flow... or give in and do nothing. Allowing your manifestations to come to you through alignment and sheer power of will.

This means graciously enabling synchronicity to guide you through the complex corridors of life. Above all, have fun, and do not become upset when things don't go your way, or when you've made a wrong turn or hit a snag in the road. Rather, exercise patience, as the game feels rather seamless once you've truly mastered how to play.

Plus, it's no coincidence that you've chanced upon these words. Which means that at some level you've attracted this knowledge, now dangling coyly at your fingertips, inviting you to continue on. When you grapple and begin to implement the principles shared in the lines that follow, life as you know it will noticeably transform.

So, if ready to play consciously– let us begin, starting with the first law...

*Which is that you Exist.* In fact, the game of life would not ensue without you, requiring each player; pawn, castle or knight to take its rightful place on the cosmic board of existence. If ever a player is missing, how then is the game to subsist?

Though, be forewarned. This game is a tad different, in that no player ever dies. Each player when tired, to the point where the body's not up to par with the mission, simply moves on to a different plane in due time. Even so, each is a winner, having fulfilled their cosmic purpose, because success is not hinged on your capacity survive.

There is no last man standing, or winner takes all. Granted you are your own judge and jury; gauging your prowess not just on your ability to fulfill your earthly agenda, but the caliber of life lived. For every act of service that uplifts another befits the whole of Creation – heedless of its scale.

To be clear, there's no sidestepping your mission by prematurely quitting the game. In fact, those that commit suicide, shortly after will find themselves transitioning, right back unto the board. Albeit it may well be a different one, having to replay the life.

So, if you imagined that you get to pick up where you left off, you may be in for a rude awakening. There are no guarantees. For while some may narrowly escape the grim fate of starting over – the so-called near-death experience, others are less inclined. In that, an attempt to exit prematurely may land you right back at the starting point.

Yet do not fret, as given that time is an illusion, there's no risk of failure, falling behind, or trailing miserably in the rear. You can get back into the game as many times as you care, as you exist perpetually. So, what is there to fear?

In truth, no soul ever perishes. So even if you were to jump into the deepest abyss or free fall from the highest cliff, the indestructible aspect of your being will prevail. This is not an invitation to test this law, unless you insist. In which case, no one will deter you, because you have free will.

You see, all is energy, and everything in the Universe including you, is in a constant state of flux. Which underpins the second law, *the Law of Perpetual Transmutation of Energy*, that asserts that nothing can be created or destroyed, but simply changes form. So, if unhappy with the deck of cards dealt with in life, you may easily swap them for a better hand next round.

In this way, you're never perpetually in a runt. For one small move, however insignificant, has the power to radically transform the outcome of the game. You hold the power to transmute any plight or predicament. Yet you must believe it just the same.

Do you see how all the other players are eyeing you with their hawkish glances, all antsy, attempting to second guess your every move? Even in the silence, there's much that's being conveyed – language being large nonverbal, a sigh, a twitch, the electric charge of a wary thought. Picking up on these subtle cues subliminally, even if this communication is not consciously apparent to you.

Owing to the very fact that we're connected, and as such, each player on the board can't help but be impacted by your every move. With, the greatest myth being that we're separate from each other, and that another exists apart from you.

Which brings us to the *Law of Unity and Divine Oneness*. For as much as the leaves and stems are not isolated from, and remain part of the whole plant, you're no less connected to the collective psyche.

When you truly embody this principle, you'll find it challenging to look at another without seeing them as an extension of yourself, or judge or inflict harm upon them, without sharing in their distress. When a root is uprooted mercilessly from the ground, or bark of a tree chopped to make firewood, isn't the entire tree affected as well?

Let's just say, you can mistreat others without wincing, or a shred of remorse. You'll no doubt reap what you sow – as all in energy. Your thoughts and deeds hold a specific frequency that spirals out into the Universe, attracting back circumstances and people that are on the same wavelength. There is no sidestepping this reciprocity, which some call karma, but is simply how the third law... *the Law of Attraction* works.

This law works in tandem with the fourth and final law, *the Law of Vibration,* as the two are closely interlinked. The fact is, we exist in a vibrational universe, and as such, that which is liken unto itself is drawn. That is not necessarily a bad thing.

Knowing this, you can then manipulate the game in your favor, attracting the desired outcome simply by paying attention to how you feel, moment to moment. Being not so concerned with what others are doing or thinking, as often it's a mask. It is the perfect decoy, to throw off your defenses and get you to react in a way that pleases them.

Hence the term poker face, for those players whose mannerisms do little to reveal the way they feel inside, as the Universe responds not to how you are being, but how you are feeling. While you may be able to manipulate your expression, energy never lies.

The highest frequency is that of truth and love. Knowing this, would you opt to play the game with integrity, treating others and the earth with compassion and care? Believe me, there's plenty of pickings to go around, if you'd just take time to notice the multitude of things before you to appreciate. So, refrain from moping about, feeling the game to be rigged – though not in your favor, and that somehow life is unfair.

Keep in mind, it was never meant to be a seamless game... a smooth ride. There's very little growth in that. However, the game is set to peak high and low, burn hot and cold, feel grounded one instant and challenging the next – highly temperamental, much like the elements of nature. Yet isn't it the volatility of the game that keeps you riveted, and coming back?

Without the contrast, how are you to appreciate the rich context within which you're playing, and the sheer perfection of the orchestration at hand?

Henceforth, allow nature to guide you, revealing much about your innate landscape, flowing freely – not unlike the elements of nature. There's less wheeling and dealing, and life becomes an effortless ride, when you no longer feel the need to manipulate and control the game, with your elaborate ruses and plans.

## <u>21</u>

# *An Elemental Plan*

In fact, the best plan is to have little – or no plans!

I know. It's a tough nut to chew on. For a part of you may feel called to action, to put into practice all that you now know. Mentally contriving, down to every minute detail, the ins and outs of each elaborate scheme on your checklist of things to act upon.

Which is not to say – you're to do away with your fancies; the version of yourself you dream of becoming, or ideals of the people you'd like to rendezvous with and meet. But do such endeavors require a tirelessly crafted agenda... all that rigor and routine?

What if I were to tell you that there's already a blueprint in place? One that was crafted and conceived prior to you incarnating into this physical realm, filled with all the guidelines you'll ever need to navigate each nook and cranny of this earthly plane.

As again, your higher mind always sees the big picture and plan. Hence, the only pretext for an alternate plan is to ease the misgivings of a crotchety ego, that struggles to submit and trust – for fear of coming undone.

It throws up all kinds of contingencies, that in effect take you out of the present moment. Yet ironically, it's only by being present can that which is lined up and awaiting you, make itself apparent.

Being present, and above all being yourself, as you're a human being not a human doing. Still, you have free will to plough away tirelessly or allow the Universe to do its part, submitting gentle effort only when needed to move the physical manifestation along. Moreover, never straining – as all struggle is unnatural and pulls you off balance, affirming scarcity and lack.

Plus, you need balance, if you're to navigate your inner and outer worlds optimally. The perfect blend of Yin and Yang energy, as too much of anything is indeed unsettling. So, allow yourself to ebb and flow in a manner that feels natural, looking to the below elements of nature; earth, water, fire, air and ether – to teach you how to be.

..........................................

In Sanskrit, *Pritvi* stands for earth. It represents fertility, stability and grounding. When you are grounded, the external circumstances of your life may ebb and flow, or even be turbulent, but who you are at the core remains unchanged. Allow the trees to teach you the art of grounding, for while the branches and leaves may sway and in the wind, the tree nonetheless remains deeply rooted – firmly anchored within.

The quickest and surest way to achieve this state is to stand barefoot on the earth. Also, incorporating a daily practice of meditation, as you'll find meditation to be most effective at harmonizing and grounding the chakra points. This doesn't mean sitting for hours on end or even sitting, as a simple walking meditation will suffice. You may also try other calming practices that provide a sense of stability and much-needed respite.

In astrology, the earth signs – namely Taurus, Virgo and Sagittarius, tend to be grounded, practical and down-to-earth. While too much of this element may present as a sluggish body and being overly sensual and attached, too little may present as being divorced from physical reality, overly abstract in one's thinking and somewhat detached.

....................................

In Sanskrit, *Jala* stands for water. It represents fluidity, adaptability and change. As you navigate life, allow yourself to be fluid, to flow and not be too rigid in your definitions. For there are many that inadvertently shut themselves away within an inescapable fortress forged upon unwavering beliefs and air-tight philosophies – that soon prove their undoing. They may dig themselves out of one box, only to find themselves in another even larger box, with little or no opening.

This is never the goal, as in every nanosecond, you are changing. So, ensure never to fixate on any 'one' understanding of a thing, nor hold too tight to steely definitions about who you are. Doing so, constrains the space for you to seamlessly evolve and expand to the highest version of yourself, which is after all – a being without limits.

In astrology, the water signs – namely Cancer, Scorpio and Pisces, tend to be imaginative, mysterious and profound. It's an element that is very quiet and calming, unless overwhelmed. It's brought back into balance by introspective practices like Yin yoga, though water-based exercises may also be of help. While too much of this element may present as being hyper-active and overly focused on the external world, too little may lead to a loss of self-awareness and being notably withdrawn.

.........................................

In Sanskrit, *Tejas* stands for fire. It represents energy, inspiration and passion. Allow the spark of who you are to fully ignite by acting on those things that feel blissful and fun. Which may not entail a trip to the moon or jet-setting on a yacht. Even so, there's no point in mulling over that which is not readily actionable. So, start small and trust that these little bouts of inspired action – will prove a useful steppingstone.

Live this way, allowing yourself to fully savor all the emotions that you are privy to experience in this earthly life. Feel everything, yet never dim your light. For doing so will no doubt fan the flame of creativity, leaping and capering on the walls of your consciousness, that even now is jockeying to be expressed and voiced.

In astrology, the fire signs, namely Aries, Leo and Sagittarius, tend to be outgoing and passionate. While too much of this element may show up as excessive ambition with a propensity to take risks, too little may present as, low drive and morale with little or no zest. For such a person, life may feel empty and mundane. Yet nothing that a spell of sungazing, and creative pursuits like gardening, art and dance cannot fix.

........................................

In Sanskrit, *Vayu* stands for air. It represents movement, expansion and communication. Become like air, formless and free flowing, offloading all that feels cumbersome and leaves you depleted and drained. Moreover, allow the air to teach you lightness of being. It's undoubtedly a feat to be able to drift with the current, and deftly sidestep the emotional snares. The obligation and guilt that will, at every turn attempt to hoodwink you into assuming a burden that was never yours to bear.

In this way, emulate the air, flowing through the room like a breath of fresh air. Leave in your wake an aroma of freshness. Never attempting to fit in with a crowd, as while others may not heed your presence, they'll certainly notice when you're not there.

In astrology, air signs – namely Gemini, Libra and Aquarius, tend to be adventurous and adaptable. While too much of this element may present as having too many thoughts and being high-strung, too little may lead to a loss of creativity and feelings of boredom. Though nothing a bit of breathwork and fresh air cannot quell.

.....................................

In Sanskrit, *Akasha* stands for ether. It represents emptiness, consciousness and intuition. Allow the ether to teach you silence and stillness, creating a sanctuary within yourself that is free of the mundane noise and distractions of the external world. More so, pay heed to those readily overlooked spaces, that straddle the distance between physical objects and hang suspended between words.

It's in the stillness and silence that you will find yourself, as there's much that lingers there. When you're not so focused on the physical that you miss the subtle cues from the other dimensions existing alongside yours, of which you're often unaware.

While too much of this element may present as feeling light-headed and spacey, a deficiency may manifest as being stubborn and willful – perhaps even a tad stony.

Imbalances that natheless may be eased, with the use of sound and aroma therapies.

You see, while these elements may complement each other, a deficit or excess of any one can overwhelm and imbalance the whole. Hence, integration and balance are pivotal. For it is only by harmonizing internally, are you able to transcend the illusions of the physical and tap into the highest frequency that is the core vibration of your soul.

In other words, if you were to remain as rooted as the earth, fluid and adaptable as water, impassioned as fire, light and unfettered as air, and open to all possibilities within the ether – wouldn't you be better able to tackle the ups and down of your world?

This being the case, would you rather be lost in the sauce, planning and tending to your outer reality, or choose instead to water and nurture your inner reality? In so doing, the right path will reveal itself to you and everything will fall into place?

# 22

# The Path is Within

The right path! The words are uttered in a voice ladened with exasperation.

What is this path anyway? Is it up... down, right, left? How can I tell if I'm even on it and haven't veered off course – adrift and unhinged from all the mocking about to where things feel a bit akilter, somewhat askew and astray?

Moreover, how can I say with certainty that I'm following my intuition and heeding the promptings of my soul, and that the voice ceded to isn't that of the ego? Driven by its unchecked whims and impulses, and insatiable appetite for control.

A barrage of questions spews forth, as if finally breaking free from a levee of repressed curiosity and cooped-up patience that had been momentarily holding them in.

They tumble forth vehemently over each other, like a squad of hockey players, jockeying to be seen and heard. The entire Universe bearing witness to your lament.

Rest assured you are heard, though the question itself may be somewhat old and archaic. With so many that have awakened asking this very question, invariably seeking clues to this perplexing quandary. Yet, the answer is much simpler than you'd imagine.

That is, to follow the breadcrumbs scattered upon the trail by your cosmic team by doing more of the things that bring you joy. More so, when in doubt and feeling lost, look for the not-so-obscure signposts and angelic codes. They are there to affirm that you are on the right path. I guarantee you; these synchronous missives are no decoy.

Though, this is not an open invitation to go hunting for them, as they're meant to be subtle cues. In that, the key intent of any guide or mentor is to point the way, so that you are to a larger degree dependent on yourself, and not to wholly chaperon you.

Bear in mind that your primary guide remains your intuition or higher self. And you'll know the direction it's prodding you in, by the waves of excitement felt – that has you giddy with excitement one minute and cavorting like a show horse the next.

This said, it would be unrealistic to imagine that you're continually in such an elated state. In fact, more often than not, you may feel pretty neutral. Still, you should be able to discern what feels most thrilling in each instant. It may manifest as someone you're drawn to, an activity that makes your heart flutter, and any manner of things.

Excitement, you'll find, serves as your own personal compass to aid you in navigating the turbulent seas within this earthy terrain. Even so, it's not a sea that flows apart from you. You see, the path being sought is not external to you, but one that emanates within. So, to navigate its unchartered waters, you must first turn inwards, and willfully still the eddies and currents therein. In the resultant calm, the path before you will become clearer. Can you imagine a better outset or rung from which to begin?

There are various rungs on this infinite ladder, allowing you to steadily ascend. With each rung climbed, inching you not necessarily closer, but allowing you more access to yourself. As shared, it was never about the destination or goal. But more about you coming to a place of acceptance within you, to where you're able to more fully, authentically and unapologetically express your unique beingness and self.

The magic that is accessible at these higher frequency rungs is beyond the bounds of your imagination, which some may refer to as Nirvana. It opens you up to a realm of unconditional love and transcendence, as nothing can outweigh the ecstasy of finding alignment with your true self. When you do, I assure you it's quite the ride.

It's a path back to oneness... a path to love, which in every moment we're undoubtedly seeking. It serves as a magnet when we see a glimmer of this in others, as like attracts like, and love is what we're ultimately made of. Yet, we tend to discount the fact that the very thing we see in another is what we as well embody and have.

Moreover, every act is an act of love, even the ones that appear rooted in hate. The very fact that you hate another means that you feel an affinity for them, though you may now be plagued by a sense of separation from the perhaps lofty expectations held. Ideals that they were perhaps, wholly or in part – not willing or able to satisfy. For would it matter if it was someone for whom you did not care?

To illustrate. I recall when I was about seven or 8, there was a girl in my lessons class called Annette that I really cared to be friends with. Back then, I was not as adept in expressing what I wanted. So instead of saying...*Hey, I really like you. Let's be friends*, I chased her all the way from our lessons to her home threatening to beat her up, simply because the interest and affection felt – was not reciprocated.

Truth is, I never intended to follow through on this threat, as up until then, my bark was stronger than my bite. Even more, while most kids my age had gotten into a tousle or two, I had never actually gotten into a physical fight.

Nevertheless, this was the only way I could justify why I was chasing her, as at that age I did not fully grasp or understand why. Why such strong emotions had taken root in me, or why I'd seek to invalidate the very attributes within her, that moments before were esteemed. Yet, suddenly, were not so pleasing in my eyes.

Realizing later, that hate is not the antithesis of love, but a different expression of it. With hate and love being on the same spectrum – and the very emotion, proffering a means to gauge the degree of separation felt and come back into alignment with the self.

You see, the path I speak of, is not meant to be a straight one, but one punctuated by countless moments that may feel off and dispiriting, or stupefyingly complex. In these instances, it's important to recalibrate the way you feel, as it's a vibrational path, nonetheless.

With practice, the not-so-aligned moments will feel less frequent to where they'll eventually wane. Though not altogether. The contrast acts as a useful signpost to let you know when you're coming off balance. To this end, some measure of these experiences must remain. Still, they become less noticeable in your reality, by virtue of you responding differently to them.

You then become a beacon through your shining example, as the frequency of love can be quite galvanizing. Like scattered embers of coal, it ignites the hearts of those around you. Who by virtue of their proximity, can't help but be inspired and changed.

The fact is, it's not so much that there you're on a path, but that you are the path, though both notions are valid. The way to tell whether you're off or on the path is by how you feel. As, it's only by tending to your vibration and paying heed to your internal world can you be the way-shower you were intended to be, ably illuminating the way.

# 23

# Love, Light & Leadership

If you are still here, reading these pages, thank you for journeying with me through this story that we have cocreated. As shared, there are no coincidences. So, it's not by mere accident, that you picked up this book, and materialized the words on these pages.

But I didn't write them – you did!

Do you really believe that? The truth is, no two people will receive and interpret the information the same way. For the words are mere signposts, and the meaning itself is not necessarily in the letters, but in the thoughts and feelings they elicit in the reader. Which if you agree, is a highly subjective thing.

With each reader – wittingly or otherwise, selecting precisely what's needed from an array of energetic symbols purported by the very words themselves. Words that right now leap and caper in perfect orchestration before your eyes, on this very page.

They compel you to have a look... a sneak peak, or glimpse. And look you will, as indeed – how enterprising you are? Leaving for yourself a scattering of breadcrumbs; covert little messages and missives that your subconscious will have no trouble deciphering, that you've strategically strewn along the way.

While the discovery may seem fated, the awareness of your own ingenuity should come as no surprise. As even now, you're enrapt in a synchronous orchestration of your own making. Yet having awakened from your reverie, will you persist in the harebrained thinking that life is happening to you – or duly take charge of your life?

By taking charge of your thoughts, deeds and words. But moreover... taking great care to sustain your frequency, as the one that's most in control is one that's intentional in the things they give their attention to, paying heed to their inner world.

True power as shared has to do with the level of control exerted over oneself, and stems from compassion, non-judgment and love. It is that which inspires others to recognize their own divinity. It is an energy that is constructive and nourishing and uplifts and energizes those around.

Inspiring them, and oft times silently, without show, flair or pomp. When fully in touch within this type of power, your touch is the gentlest yet mightiest there is. In fact, it takes a great deal to build someone up and very little to tear them down.

The surest way to understand your own power to influence and inspire another, is through the expression of the divinity that's within. For words do not teach, experience does. So, it's only by expressing and sharing your gifts – *less talking and more doing,* can you lead by virtue of your example. To this end, others are drawn to you, not just because of who you say you are, but how you are being.

Moreover, remaining warm and caring – the walking embodiment and example of one that's virtuous and true, and treating others how you yourself care to be treated, by acknowledging the *Godforce* in all. With the recognition that every act of service and meritorious deed that benefits one – befits the whole of you.

You see – if you truly understood and accepted that we're all one and the same energy, if another wins and flourishes in the game of life, isn't this your win too?

And above all else – be true to yourself by remaining authentically you.

One that's fully in touch with who they are is most magnetic, with the power to enchant and captivate, just as a moth is drawn to a flame, and ants zealously line up to follow the crumbs scattered on a trail. Or perhaps – how you may have felt impelled, rivetingly so, to keep turning these pages.

Not quite sure what lies in store, but compelled and curious all the same. Though, the attraction lies not in the lure of the thing external... the thought-provoking words, succulent crumbs or enticing flame, but an innate sense of alignment detected within.

Bear in mind that you'll never attract or lead those that are not attuned with you. Plus, it's not necessarily your job to steer another – but yourself, as they have their own innate guidance system too. Even so, leadership results naturally when you have full dominion of who you are, as others can't help but emulate and be impacted by you.

You're a leader not because of your ability to lure and win over a bevy of followers, but rather, by your capacity to inspire others to lead themselves. So, never fall prey to the heady power trips that ensnare many a well-intended altruist. But instead act from a space of unconditionality, with little expectation of reward and repayment.

It is the strongest expression of the I AM presence, and most meritorious act of service there is. In fact, one that's aligned has the power to balance and off-set the energy of many that may feel lost, bitter and desolate, causing the collective energy to tip positively on the cosmic scale.

Still, remaining true and heart-centered may be easier said than done. Yet there's something undoubtedly magical that happens when you strip away the mask to reveal more of you and set the illusory aspects of your persona down.

In so doing, you peel away the layers, much like the petals of an eye-catching yet reticent flower, only to unveil the soft, delicate and unsullied pistil at the core. You come full circle to the realization that who you are at the core is often known only to you and your inner being. We rarely allow the world to see us – to behold our inner beauty and light, as we're too busy masking and fixating on how we're perceived on the outside.

Yet when you strip away these guises, how beautiful you are to the eye. A rare and precious flower. In truth, there's none like you. So, why mask your colors? Why dim your light? When your entire rainbow body is aching to be revealed, and raring to come online.

It's activated by love, as self-love and acceptance are key. It's key to unlocking your full potential. When unshackled, more of who you are will come into view and be revealed.

You'll come to the realization that... you are love. This is the true nature of who you are. Knowing all that you now know, can you accept this, Divine soul?

Can you finally accept the divine and magnificent being that you are?

*You are this rainbow. You are love, you are light.*
*You are so very beautiful, so very beautiful indeed.*
*~Namaste.*

# – THE END –

# About the Author

From a very early age, I felt I was different. Not special, but different. I knew it, but why didn't the world have this knowing? Or maybe they did. What was clear is that I did not see the world the same way that many did.

I remember the day, the sky changed. It was different. I could not articulate it. It was just 'a *knowing*', the kinda thing that could not be grappled with the mind. I must have been seven- or eight-years young then. Something had moved, something had shifted, something had changed. Something had been lost. Of course, nothing is ever lost, as the Universe of which we are a part, is in a constant state of evolution. But that moment was forever cemented in my mind.

I grew up in a country that was replete with superstition, and deeply conditioned beliefs that were etched in the minds of its people. People were conditioned to fear that which they could not understand. So, words like obeah and voodoo were on everyone's lips, from the slightest echo of that which went against the norm.

The norm. That which was not the norm, that existed in the absence of that which was normal. That which is abnormal.

Thence, began the indoctrination. Ghosts were seen and heard but never spoken about. Then there were the out of body experiences, I always wondered about these, as upon re-merging with the body, I was able to confirm the experiences seen; the clothing that my aunt wore and what she was doing in the kitchen moments before seeing her.

I recall walking upon the pathway that ran through the local cemetery, lined on both ends by graves set above the ground that stretched for miles as far as the eyes could see. It's a time when the sunset kissed the dark, and the smell of the perfume of bodies rotting filled the air. They have a distinct scent you know.

And all whom had been conditioned to believe in ghosts and *jumbees* scattered. Yet without a soul in sight, there was an energy emanating from the gravesite that felt strangely comforting. In the silence of the graveyard, I felt most connected with God. It was my strongest hour. Shortly thereafter, I announced to my stoutly religious family, that I was not anymore religious. I am something. I'm not sure what that thing is, but I know what it is not.

Later, I moved to the US, the land of opportunity. Much of what that quaint fortune teller said when I laughingly had her read my fortune amongst a giggling gaggle of schoolmates came to pass. Well, most everything, less the part about having kids.

Yet, in that space where it felt like I had acquired what many would consider to be the *pipedream*, I felt that there was something missing. So, I dappled in meditation, metaphysics and philosophy, and went for long walks along darkened streets peering into the windows of privileged households, wondering how they lived.

I began to look forward to these evening meanderings, as it was in those moments when I was surrounded by no-one, that I felt less alone.

In 2009, I got to experience who I am. I had just gone through one of the most identity-changing, psychologically confusing periods where everything that felt secure came crashing down; self-worth, job, friendships – you name it. With nothing left, I decided in that moment to live for myself... to re-define myself in a way that was authentic for me. Moreover, to never alter myself to fit in with the world ever again.

So, with that, I shaved my head, landed a new job, and spoke my truth with no thought or concern regarding how it would be received. Strangely, the more I spoke and lived this truth – something magical evolved. People were pulled to me, as it created space for them to show up as their true selves and express the magic that they are.

Each encounter was like weaving a story with the other, where time stood still, and the ensuing moment was imbued with presence. The mind went quiet, and the soul came alive. Before I knew it, I was living though the heart.

When that happens, it is very magical indeed. The heart expanded with a love that was not romantic, but the kind that made you feel like you're walking on air. The form of others appeared different. It was like I was seeing them in a hue of colors. This experience did not last very long; a few months – but was enough for the feeling of that version of me that I was being to imprint in my memory.

Without warning, my world came crashing down again, and I was mercilessly shoved once again into space, I ranted and swore I would never be in.

Looking back, I see how everything has unfolded in cycles. But it is not a wheel, it's more a spiral. There's a polarity and a neutral middle; and the rise and fall, the up and the down, the in and the out, the light and the dark. Each experience unfolds to provide a context to fully experience the absence or presence of that which you are experiencing, and to allow an intensity of understanding.

For it is only from hitting what felt like rock bottom, that I was able to feel fully the experience of the lightness of being. Plus, it is only by experiencing a heart that is cold and closed off, that I am amazed and dumbfounded when my heart feels like it is bursting out of my chest.

Moreover, it's by stepping through life in a body that is judged as pretty that I can fully appreciate the experience of feeling unseen. Having grown up with very little, I can also have an understanding that all is relative, and that poverty and abundance are subjective based on what is valued in life.

Finally, it is by going without that I'm able to experience the connectedness and completeness of going within – and traversing that Universe that is accessible within each of us. The Universe is not truly outside of us; there's an entire world within that is imperceptible to five senses. As above so below. As without so within. The Universe stretches in all directions, with each path bringing you closer to what you are.

*To stay connected with Natasha and her offerings, visit: www.ascend5d.com*

*May your path be filled with remembrance and light*

# Addendum

Why? Did you imagine that this was just another book to be read from cover to cover and stowed away to gather dust in some musty corner of your world? If so, you couldn't be anymore misinformed. For once you've removed the rose-colored glasses that you've been – up 'til now, unseeingly meandering your universe with, you'll find it near impossible to put them back on.

Even so, dear reader. You may be wondering what's the next step. What's the next step along your journey... next move ahead? And, while this is not for me to say, there's nothing against me giving you a little nudge... a bit of a jump off point, if you will.

Still, no manner of learnings can make you any shrewder, as knowledge itself is quite useless, devoid of application. In so far as your reality is a physicalized one, physical action is needed, as how else are you to put into practice what you've learnt?

To this end, you'll find the following meditations and practices quite helpful.

Each build upon the other, and by design – is intended to galvanize you into action. This way, you may step powerfully into your mission, with an open heart and balanced mind. Because you have free will, you may implement these exercises, only if it tickles your heart to do so – and as needed, return to them from time to time.

# Practice 1: Stilling the Mind

Create a sanctuary within your home; a quiet place where you can step away from the noise and bustle of the outside world and will be completely undisturbed. This may be a separate room within your home, or a closet. It's my recommendation to meditate in low or no light, so this should also be a space that is somewhat sequestered from bright fluorescent lighting and sunlight.

Your attire should be loose and comfortable. Avoid any garments with elastic banding that hug the waist, or that is close fitting. It is also suggested that your garment be made of natural fabrics, for clothing like everything else carries a specific frequency. Cotton and linen will suffice. Light and neutral colors are also advised.

Make yourself comfortable. You may sit cross-legged on a cushion, chair or stool maintaining an erect spine, or lie on a yoga mat. Whatever position feels most relaxed.

Your hands too – place them in the position that feels most natural. Below are a few common mudra practices for your reference. Try them out to see which one fits best.

- *Apana mudra*: This mudra is known to aid digestion and promote the release of toxins from your system. Touch the tips of the thumb, ring and middle fingers, with the palm facing upwards, while keeping the remaining fingers outstretched.

- *Bhairava mudra*: This mudra is known to promote deep reflection and fosters a sense of security and inner peace. Place the right palm within the left and allow your hands to rest gently on your lap if sitting, or on your stomach if lying down.

- *Chinmaya mudra:* This is a very grounding mudra that is very effective at calming the mind and soothing the nervous system. Touch the tips of the thumb and index fingers, with the palm facing downwards and the remaining fingers outstretched.

- *Dhyana mudra*: This mudra allows for intense focus and promotes deep meditation. Place the right hand on top of the left, interlacing the fingers and allowing the thumbs to lightly touch. Allow the palms to face upwards, with your hands resting gently on your lap. Doing so closes the energetic circuit of the body.

- *Gyan mudra*: This mudra is known to enhance wisdom and knowledge, while promoting a feeling of balance and calm. Touch the tip of your thumbs and index fingers together, with the remaining fingers extended out. You may rest your hands on your legs if seated cross-legged, or along your sides if lying down.

- *Prana mudra:* This mudra is known to revitalize your lifeforce energy or chi. Allow the tips of the pinky and ring fingers to gently touch the tip of the thumb, with the palm facing upwards and remaining fingers outstretched.

- *Prithvi mudra:* This mudra is known to reduce stress and promote healing, stability and calm. Allow the tip of your thumb to gently touch the ring finger, with your palms facing upwards, and the remaining fingers outstretched.

- *Shunya mudra:* This mudra is known to promote a state of tranquility by balancing the ether element of the body. Touch the tips of the thumb to the middle finger, with the palm facing upwards and remaining fingers outstretched.

You may also light a candle or incense stick, as you may find these to be most soothing, or play soft, ambient music in the background. However, if you are a beginner, my recommendation is that you start without any sounds.

When you are ready – start by inhaling deeply through the right nose and exhaling completely through the mouth three times, and alternate nostril. This practice of breathing prior to meditation relaxes the body and synchronizes the left and right hemispheres of the brain.

Now close your eyes. Breathe normally.

Do not seek – for what will come next. Be still. Allow the thoughts and concerns of the day to fall away.

As thoughts arise, do not struggle to tamp them down, but allow down to gently fade like clouds adrift within your consciousness. Imagine each as a whisp of cloud, nimbly floating away.

Just like you would discipline a small child that is acting out, do not pay them any mind. With repeated practice, the mind will eventually acquiesce and be still. If you're new to meditation, this may take a bit of time.

As you continue to sit or lie, you may feel the urge to squirm or feel an itch. Or your legs may feel cramped, achy and stiff. To the degree possible, notice these sensations, without succumbing to the impulse to shift position or relieve the itching. In time, these sensations that are a result of the energy shifts within the body, will melt away.

Focus your gaze on the third eye, the area right between your brows. Notice the space that is there.

This space may be initially dark and devoid of light, but with practice, you may start to notice orbs of light or subtle colors or shapes. Allow yourself to notice them, without ascribing any meaning to them.

As the conscious mind relaxes, in the resultant stillness – you may receive various bits of information, mental images and visuals, audible messages, noticeable smells and sensations in various parts of the body. Do not attempt to analyze what you're seeing or otherwise sensing with the logical mind. Just allow what's coming through to be.

It is recommended that you repeat this practice daily, or at the very least a few times per week. If you are new to meditation, you may start out with 15 minutes, and gradually increase the duration. It takes most people on average 15 minutes to calm and hush the mental chatter of the mind.

Keep a journal near to record any insights that may come up during the practice.

# Practice 2: Clearing & Balancing the Chakras

Find a place where you can sit or lie comfortably, relatively undisturbed. While it's perfectly fine to lie down, you'll find that you'll get the most benefit sitting on a stool or chair with your feet flat on the ground.

Set an intention for the practice, in this case, to clear and balance your chakras.

When you are ready – close your eyes and take three to six deep breaths in through your nose, exhaling through the mouth. Do this at your own pace, pausing to hold the air in your lungs following the inhale for 2-3 seconds, prior to exhaling. All the while, keeping the head, neck and chest as immobile as you can.

On the final exhale, envision a ball of white light at the base of your root chakra, steadily moving up your spine. See the ball moving through each of your chakra, clearing and energizing each in turn. Visualize each chakra as follows:

- Root Chakra: See this as a red, lotus shaped flower
- Sacral Chakra: See this as orange, lotus shaped flower
- Solar Plexus: See this as yellow, lotus shaped flower
- Heart Chakra: See this as green, lotus shaped flower
- Throat Chakra: See this as blue, lotus shaped flower
- Third Eye Chakra: See this as deep indigo, lotus shaped flower
- Crown Chakra: See this as purple, lotus shaped flower

Bear in mind that on the final exhale you are not letting the air out of your mouth but rather, keeping the mouth closed and allowing the momentum and pressure of the resultant air to build up within you.

This in kind, forces the sacred secretion of cerebrospinal fluid that ordinarily cycles through your system about four times daily, to move up through the spine. This helps to restore not only balance to the chakras, but to your entire system – as a whole.

Repeat this exercise three times. Allow the ball to cycle out of the top of your crown, down the front of your body and reenter the base of the root chakra, with each turn. Next, visualize this very ball of light extending upwards through the crown chakra and radiating out into the cosmos – merging with all that is, for the 3rd and final round.

Now breathe normally. As you inhale, imagine breathing fresh revitalizing energy into each chakra, and upon the exhale... letting go of stale used-up energy from each respective energy center. Do this with each chakra, in turn.

As you move through the various energy centers, allow your attention to linger momentarily upon each chakra point. Bring the light of your awareness to each, while repeating the following affirmations quietly in your mind.

- Root Chakra: I AM rooted
- Sacral Chaka: I AM creative
- Solar Plexus: I AM powerful and strong
- Heart Chakra: I AM love
- Throat Chakra: I AM truth
- Third Eye Chakra: I AM clear sighted
- Crown Chakra: I AM divine

At the conclusion of the exercise, spend a few minutes in silence with your eyes closed, noticing how your body feels, and any sensations that may arise from each of these focal points. You may stay in this mediation posture, for as long as is necessary, giving space and time for the energy within each center to settle and subside. As a benchmark, five to ten minutes is usually enough time. Moreover, do keep a journal close to notate and track any impressions or insights that might arise.

In short, you'll find this practice to be very grounding and calming. To extract the most benefit, I recommend alternating it with your regular meditation routine. Perform it weekly or biweekly, in instances where you feel unstable and stressed, and when experiencing fluctuations with your weight or severe fatigue.

# Practice 3: Activating the Pineal Gland

Get into a meditation posture. The use of ambient music in the background is quite suitable for this practice. Now set the intention to activate your pineal gland, optionally calling upon your guides and angels to aid and assist you, if you so wish.

Close your eyes. When ready, take a few deep breaths, and allow your body to relax. On the final breath, bring your middle and index fingers to the area of your third eye – the point located between your brows, and lightly tap this area maintaining a steady rhythm for about 2 to 3 minutes.

As you tap it, notice any sensations that may arise. You may notice subtle lights or colors, or the energy in this area may palpably shift. Hold space for whatever arises, neither attempting to analyze or attribute meaning to what is seen or felt.

Continue to breathe, focusing on the sensation of the air entering and leaving the center of your forehead, on each inhale and exhale. At your own pace, bring your arms back into a relaxed position, resting them along your sides or gently on your legs.

Now, return your awareness to the third eye. See this energy center as a rotating orb of indigo light, vibrant and bright. Next, visualize a beam of white light moving into this chakra – cleansing and clearing it, as you would a clogged pipe.

An intense stream of light, entering this chakra point and illuminating it from within, and charging this center, so that it pulses and vibrates. Allow yourself to tune into the sensation of the luminous energy orbiting within its midst.

If unable to feel this energy, shift your attention slightly outwards to hover in the air just above your forehead, as if doing this exercise for the 1st time, you may find it easier to pick up on the sensations orbiting there.

Now inhale deeply, and upon the exhale, direct this energy down through your body into your abdomen or out through the soles of your feet – to diffuse the energy and avoid overstimulating your head.

Remain in the meditation posture for another five to ten minutes, and notice what impressions come up – if any. Notate these afterwards within your journal, as even if the meaning is not readily apparent, in time it may become clear.

# Practice 4: Healing the Inner Child

Retrieve a picture of yourself as a kid. It should be a picture that you are extremely fond of, that serves as a representation of your younger self – the little you that has amassed a myriad of beliefs, based on countless experiences it has had.

If those experiences were positive and affirmative, you likely have a heathy opinion of yourself. On the contrary, if those experiences were traumatic, you may be holding on to core underlying beliefs that you're not worthy or deserving of love.

Create a sacred space within your home or on your person to house this picture; a place that's readily accessible where you may see it at a glance. This may be on your nightstand beside your bed, in your wallet or other such place, close at hand.

Grab a pen and paper, and section the paper in two. On one side, make a list of the top – say five or six, things that you love about yourself, and on the other, the things you disdain or perhaps do not like quite as much. For instance, you may not currently appreciate some aspect of your body or consider yourself smart enough. Yet on the other hand, may know yourself to be kind and empathetic, with an artistic flair and touch.

Now go through each of the not-so-positive attributes and attempt to recall the first time you felt that way. Was it a feeling that stemmed from your childhood, or belief acquired as an adult? If so, what specifically triggered this lack-based thought? Was it something unkind someone said to you, perhaps a family member or friend? Or an opinion deduced based on how those around you treated you, and what was observed.

Take for instance, you were repeatedly chastised for being plain or ugly, and told that you'll never amount to anything as you're slow-witted and daft. And believed this to be true. Isn't this just the perspective of another that's projecting their own sense of unworthiness upon you. What reason then do you have, to take their opinion as fact?

People are often quick to ridicule that which they perceive as different. But so, what if you're different? You're not here to blend in just so they can feel comfortable, and most definitely – not here to assume their trauma-based programming as your own.

Now speak to this picture, this inner child of yours as you would speak to any kid in your care, relying upon your protection, and desiring to be reassured of your love. Let it know that you see it, and that there's so much about him or her you adore. Say out loud the positive qualities previously cited, assuring it that there's nothing that needs to change as it is worthy just as it is. And believe this.

Next, apologize to your inner child – saying to it, that you're sorry for every instance that you yourself criticized or berated it, did not stand up for and amply defend it, or allowed others to mistreat him or her. Moreover, forgive yourself, especially now that you know better, and will demonstrate this knowing, starting now.

The following mediation may be used in conjunction with the above exercise. It is intended as a one-off practice. However, you may return to it, on occasion, if or when childhood issues resurface, and you have the urge to console your inner child.

Find a quiet space, indoors or outdoors, that is free of distraction and relatively quiet. Make yourself comfortable, by either sitting cross-legged, or on a stool or bench with your feet flat on the floor. Take a deep breath through your nose, hold it for a few seconds, and exhale through your mouth. Do this six times.

Now recall a time when you were younger, when you may have felt powerless, alone or afraid. Visualize the childhood home you were living in back then. Imagine standing outside of the building and looking at it. Picture it in as much detail as possible; the color, shape, and any key features that come to mind.

Next, enter the door of your childhood home, and head into the room that you stayed in – perhaps alone, or with a sibling or parent. See the room empty, and exactly as you remember it, recognizing the bed you slept in, the walls and ceiling, and any of your favorite memorabilia from back then.

Take a moment to look around the room, allowing your eyes to rest upon the closet. If there wasn't one, imagine a closet located in the far corner of the room.

Now make your way over to the closet, and slowly open the door. Sitting on the floor of the closet is your younger self... a little boy or girl that looks exactly as you did back then. The hair, the skin color, the eyes, even the clothing is the same.

The child is looking up at you with eyes wide and expressive. You can tell it's troubled and needs solace. Now stoop to kneel in front of this child and wrap your arms around it, saying to it, all the things you wish someone had said to you back then.

Reassure the child that you love it, and that it's never alone, as you're always there watching over and protecting it. Let him or her know how beautiful he or she is. That every aspect of it is beautiful and unique, and that it no longer needs to hide itself away from the world.

Notice how its face lights up upon hearing your words – and promise. See the trust that wells up in its eyes, just from knowing that from now on, you'll never again neglect it. Tune into how light your heart feels, and in this uplifted state, make your way out of the house, the very way you came in.

Now at your own pace, allow your consciousness to return to the space where you are right now sitting. Notice the sensations around you; the way the ground feels beneath your feet and legs. When ready, slowly come back to the present moment.

# Practice 5: Body Sensing Technique

As you now know – in every moment your cells are speaking to you, if you are tuned in enough to hear. Yet we've been so conditioned to overlook these sensations, running to the nearest doctor, which is not to say that such practitioners do not serve a purpose, rather than allow our innate self-healing mechanisms to prevail.

As within, so without. Every external manifestation, regardless of appearance, be it agreeable or lamentable, serves as an indicator of the body's internal state. We can better care for and nurture our divine temple, when we start to recognize these external cues, evidenced in the following examples. Moreover, by heeding what our cells are attempting to convey to us, we can nip such pesky ailments in the bud.

In so doing, we can address the root cause of such issues, regardless of where in the body they may crop up. Though location is nonetheless relevant, with ailments on the right indicative of the underlying stressors and botherations that are right now in your life. Whereas those on the left side of the body are rooted in things, long past – that even now may linger, seeking your reflection and resolve.

Starting with the body's form....

Body Form: A person that slouches backwards when walking may find life overall to be a bit overwhelming, and as such – rather than lean into life and take risks, may cower from it. On the contrary, a person that feels a sense of lack or scarcity may slouch forward, constantly leaning into life. Often, pushing that which is lined up for them away, with the intense desperation felt. On the same token, one that is hunched in may have gotten used to dimming their light and making themselves small. So over time the body starts to cave in on itself, starved of a much-needed creative expression and outlet.

Shoulders: Aches and pains in the shoulders may be indicative of the person shouldering the weight of issues that aren't theirs to bear. Such a person may disregard their soul's agenda, to further the agenda of another. Or perhaps – care too much about the opinions and perception of the external world, giving little importance to their own.

Neck: Maladies of the neck may be indicative of one in the habit of suppressing their voice and truth, for fear of being judged. This may also be suggestive of rigidity, and a lack of flexibility when engaging with the external world. As well as dogmatic beliefs held that may shackle their and expansion, inadvertently holding them back.

Eyes: Ailments of the eye may be indicative of a lack of focus or being focused on the things that are not aligned. In so doing, they may navigate the world unseeingly, and as such – miss the many signs and cues that have been placed in your view. Telltale clues that they would otherwise benefit from, if they didn't overlook them each time.

Legs and Feet: Issues in the legs and feet are indicative of one that is not well-grounded or may be feeling stuck. Such a person may feel like they are not moving forward in their life's purpose. Too timid to take a leap in the direction of that which excites them and act on the soul's agenda, with the issue arising to garner their attention and give them a bit of pluck.

While a detailed discussion on such bodily cues is beyond the scope of this book, the above examples shared, is merely to whet your appetite. Moreover, to encourage a more expanded and holistic way of viewing your body, that again is always in communion with you, if you'd only have the wherewithal to tune in and take heed.

In this vein, the following meditative practice is intended to shift your focus inwards and sets the stage for you to begin to tune in and become acquainted with your cells – the innate part of your physical being.

Find a quiet space within which to meditate, where you'll be relatively undisturbed. Soft, ambient music in the background may be helpful, if you find the sounds soothing, and they aide you to relax. You may choose to sit upright with an erect spine, or lie flat – whatever feels most apt.

Once comfortable, take a few deep breaths, inhaling through the nose and exhaling completely through the mouth, to relax the body and calm the mind. Now place your hands in laps or whatever mudra feels befitting, and gently close your eyes.

Allow your attention to move to the top of your head, noticing the sensation at the center of your crown. Do not attempt to assign meaning to what you feel. Notice if the energy in this part of your body feels dense or airy. Now, breathe in deeply, allowing the breath to travel all the way to the crown. Hold your breath, then relax.

Next, allow your attention to travel to the area of the face, noticing the sensations within your face. Tune into how this area of your body feels. Notice if there is any tingling, or discomfort there. Breathe in deeply, allowing the breath to travel all the way to the cells within your face – feeling them come alive and reinvigorated, then relax.

Next, allow your attention to travel to the area at the back of your head, noticing the sensations there. Tune into how this area of your body feels. Notice the temperature of the cells in this area. Are they warm? Are they perhaps cool? Breathe in deeply, allowing the breath to travel all the way to the back of your head, then relax.

Next, allow your attention to travel to the area of the neck, noticing the sensations there. Tune into how the cells in this area of your body feel. Do they perhaps feel stiff and congested? Breathe in deeply, allowing the breath to travel all the way to the area of your neck. Hold your breath, then relax.

Next, allow your attention to travel to the area of the chest, noticing the sensations there. Tune into how the cells in this area of your body feel. Are there any sensations that stand out? Breathe in deeply, allowing the breath to travel all the way to the area of your chest, then relax.

Next, allow your attention to travel to the area of the shoulders, noticing the sensations there. Notice if there is any tension in this area. Breathe in deeply, allowing the breath to travel all the way to the area of your shoulders. Hold the inhale for a few seconds, allowing any signs of tension to melt away, then relax.

Next, allow your attention to travel to your arms and hands, noticing the sensations there. Notice how the cells in this area of your body feel. Do you notice a tingling sensation there? Breathe in deeply, allowing the breath to travel through your arms all the way to the tips of your fingers, then relax.

Next, allow your attention to travel to the area of your torso, noticing the sensations there. Breathe in deeply, feeling the power of your breath expand and energize the cells in your abdomen with each inhale. Now breathe out and relax.

Next, allow your attention to travel to legs and thighs, noticing the sensations there. Tune into how the cells in this area of your body feel. Do they feel strained and tight? Breathe in deeply, allowing the breath to travel all the way to the area of your lower limbs, and relax.

Next, allow your attention to travel to feet, noticing any sensations there. Notice if there is any tension in this area. Now breathe in deeply, allowing any such sensations to melt away. Hold your breath at the top of the exhale, then relax.

Now, bring your consciousness back to the present moment. Take a few minutes to jot down any distinct impressions and sensations felt in the body, reflecting on each. See if any insights come up intuitively and notate these as well. You may return to this practice whenever you're feeling out of touch, disconnected from your body or ill at ease.

With practice, you'll be better attuned to picking up on the subtle cues that your body is giving you, so that you may promptly act upon them. In so doing, you'll become more synchronized with the whole of you.

# Practice 6: Enhancing your Personal Power

You were never meant to be a victim or villain in your story, so let's rewrite the play. It's a very short one. Though, it's not a script about mastering your emotions to appear more mysterious nor manipulating others to feel less vulnerable, secure and safe.

In fact, it has little to do with having dominion of others. And all to do with recognizing the things innate to the self that you have true control of and loosening your grip of everything else. For power over others, is really weakness disguised as strength.

Most paramount among the things in your command, is the level of regard and light in which you view yourself. A light that can be rather dazzling when you wholly embrace your truth, leading to you embodying a more authentic and empowered expression of the self. A version that you may begin to embody, starting now.

For this practice, you'll utilize the worksheets included at the end of this section.

Now choose a 6-hour window in the day, when you're most likely to interact with the outside world. Next, get ready for the fun part, as this will require a bit of self-monitoring, though not in any strict way... of your thought and deed and word.

Week 1: Notice any instances within the selected window when you've done something against your wishes just to please another, or from you wanting to avoid conflict. Perhaps you were too scared to disagree, say no and turn them down.

- Identify three such people pleasing actions and write them down in the 1st column.

- Now, in the adjacent column – for each action cited, include a correction action and plan. It should be a realistic action that you'll implement the next time you find yourself in a similar position. I say realistic, as this does not mean turning down a work assignment given to you by a manager, knowing fully well the company foots your bills. So be savvy about this.

- Continue to monitor your actions daily, until the opportunity to implement the action plan presents itself. Make sure to designate the action as complete, only once you've successfully executed the plan.

- Once complete, note in your journal – how it feels to ditch the people-pleasing tendencies that are not aligned with your highest conduct. Do you feel more empowered? Perhaps more natural? Use as many descriptive adjectives as you can, keeping in mind that in so doing, you are redefining the new you.

Week 2: Notice any instances within the selected window when you've said or uttered something insincere just to manipulate the way others see you. This includes agreeing with them when you have a different opinion or failing to voice your opinion at the risk of sounding peevish or being wrong. Or perhaps – when you flat out lied to conceal something deemed unfavorable, ruinous or wrong.

- Identify three such untrue statements and write them down in the 1st column.
- Now, in the adjacent column – for each statement cited, include a correction action and plan. Again, make it realistic, as this increases the likelihood of the challenge you've set for yourself getting done.
- Continue to monitor your words daily, until the opportunity to implement the action plan presents itself. Designate the action as complete, only once you've successfully executed the plan.
- Once complete, note in your journal – how it feels to ditch the insincere words that are not aligned with your highest truth. Do you feel more

transparent? Perhaps more honorable? Use as many descriptive adjectives as you can, keeping in mind that in so doing, you are redefining the new you.

Week 3: Notice any instances within the selected window when you've held a self-demeaning thought about yourself. This one should be a piece of cake, as we tend to be our own worst critics.

- Identify three such thoughts and write them down in the 1st column.
- Now, in the adjacent column – for each thought cited, replace it with a new, more helpful thought, by asking yourself the following questions.
- Is this thought wholly true?
- Is this thought always true?
- Is this thought representative of the reality that I seek to create?
- Once complete, note in your journal – how it feels to ditch the self-deprecating thoughts that are not aligned with who you know yourself to be. Do you feel more uplifted? Perhaps more whole? Use as

many descriptive adjectives as you can, keeping in mind that in so doing, you are redefining the new you.

These exercises will give you a jumpstart in recognizing how through your thoughts, words and deeds, you create your reality. For you are a natural creator by nature, and personal power begins at the crossing where victimhood ends.

Knowing this, what will you create next?

SECTION A: ACTIONS

In this section, write down any people-pleasing or pacifying actions performed.

| | People Pleasing or Pacifying Actions | Corrective Action |
|---|---|---|
| 1 | | |
| 2 | | |
| 3 | | |

SECTION B: WORDS

In this section, write down any insincere or untruthful words uttered.

| | Insincere or Untruthful Words | Corrective Action |
|---|---|---|
| 1 | | |
| 2 | | |
| 3 | | |

SECTION C: THOUGHTS

In this section, write down any negative and demeaning thoughts held about yourself

| | Non-serving Thoughts | Corrective Action |
|---|---|---|
| 1 | | |
| 2 | | |
| 3 | | |